T0031383

The UN⚽FFICIAL
WORLD CUP ALBUM

The UN⚽FFICIAL
WORLD CUP ALBUM

A POORLY ILLUSTRATED INCOMPLETE HISTORY

From the 'artists' known as
NO SCORE DRAWS

Harper
North

HarperNorth
Windmill Green
Mount Street
Manchester M2 3NX

A division of
HarperCollinsPublishers
1 London Bridge Street
London SE1 9GF

www.harpercollins.co.uk

HarperCollinsPublishers
1st Floor, Watermarque Building, Ringsend Road
Dublin 4, Ireland

First published by HarperNorth in 2022

1 3 5 7 9 10 8 6 4 2

Copyright © No Score Draws and Alex Pratchett 2022
Design by Louise Leffler

No Score Draws asserts the moral right to
be identified as the author of this work

A catalogue record for this book
is available from the British Library

HB ISBN: 978-0-00-853622-0

Printed and bound in Latvia by PNB.

MIX
Paper from
responsible sources
FSC™ C007454

This book is produced from independently certified FSC™ paper
to ensure responsible forest management.

For more information visit: www.harpercollins.co.uk/green

'Praise' for the work of

NO SCORE DRAWS

'It's absolutely awful and I love it.'

'Will absolutely ruin my
partner's Christmas.'

'Splendid and horrid at the same time.'

'Were my expectations met?
Sadly, yes.'

HOW DID WE GET HERE?

It was 2014, the night before the opening game of that summer's World Cup. There was excitement, anticipation, that heady pre-tournament giddiness. And, because it was a World Cup, there was also an accompanying sticker book, and 640 lovely football stickers to fill it with. I, Alex – a lapsed child of 30 – wanted to collect them.

As a 10-year-old I'd got within half a dozen stickers of completing the USA '94 World Cup album but had been cruelly denied by pack after pack of 'gots' when I all I needed were five or six 'needs.' I'd not felt the need to waste an extraordinary proportion of my income on football stickers in the intervening decades but, seeing some like-minded friends swapping their doublers in the pub this World Cup eve, the urge to confront some unfinished childhood business bubbled to the surface.

So, over our pints, I asked my wife Sian if she'd have any objection to me pursing this silly indulgence. 'Look at their little faces,' I said, pointing across the pub at our friends as they delightedly exchanged theirs Neymars and Ronaldos Pirlos: '...they look so happy.'

They really did.

Trouble was, there was an article doing the rounds at the time saying it could potentially cost up to £450 to fill the sticker album. £450 is *loads*. And Sian had seen the article. And we were fairly skint. So, by applying maths, we quickly came to the conclusion that it wasn't really a goer. Probably more important things to spend our money on, like food and rent and what have you. Shame though.

We weren't just bad at drawing, we were offensively, objectively terrible.

And then...

And then Sian had an idea.
A stupid idea. A stupid idea that would utterly torpedo our lives.
Could we make – and fill – our own sticker album for nothing?
As in zero pounds, zero pence. 'How would we do that?' I asked.
Her reply: 'We could... draw them?'

That was her idea: draw every single World Cup 2014 Panini sticker.
Us. It is *essential* at this point to point out that we are not artists:
I could draw an 80 per cent accurate Homer Simpson, and Sian at
least had an Art 'A'-Level from circa 2001-ish but, seriously, neither
of us could draw.

With less than 24 hours until the World Cup kicked off we'd set
ourselves a little challenge: could we, two people who can't draw,
knock out all 640 stickers by the time the World Cup ended? 640
stickers in 32 days.

The next day, the hosts Brazil kicked-off the opening game against
Croatia, and we set to work. And good grief, we were even worse
than we feared. We weren't just bad at drawing, we were offensively,
objectively terrible. By the end of day one, we'd done twenty-odd of
the things. And they were uniformly awful.

But we kept going. I'd started a little Twitter account to go with the
nonsense under the moniker @CheapPanini, thinking at best it
might amuse a few friends. Suddenly, though, we had a couple of

We were now spending six hours a day drawing Cameroonian full backs.

hundred followers. Then a thousand. And then the *Guardian* got in touch and it all went mad. We were on the news in Japan. In papers in Iran and Colombia and Mexico and Brazil. Camera crews came to our house. I babbled to Simon Mayo on Radio 2, desperately trying (and failing) to explain ourselves. It was bananas. We both had *real* jobs which were tiring enough, but we were now spending six hours a day drawing Cameroonian full backs. It all got a bit much. We wanted to back out. But we were in too deep, there was no stopping now.

We ploughed on, churning out abject, dismal sticker after abject, dismal sticker. We woke up early to draw before work. We drew on our lunchbreaks. We went round to friends' houses to watch games and took our pencils. Sian went on a hen-do and interrupted her fun to sit on a beach and draw Franck Ribéry excruciatingly badly. The stickers piled up, every one lovingly stuck into our dog-eared, increasingly ridiculous homespun album. Sian started making shinies out of tin foil like the fantastic maniac that she is.

It was the maddest month of our lives. We chipped away, day after day. The drawings resolutely failed to improve but, slowly but surely, we inched our way towards completion. We staggered across the line, finishing the last sticker mere minutes before the Final kicked off, to a small fanfare of cheers from our assembled friends.

And that was that.

Only, it wasn't.

Because stupidly, two years later Euro 2016 rolled round, and people poked and prodded us to do it again. So, we did, but this time to raise money for charity. Mystifyingly, we raised over £4000. And then two years after that, World Cup 2018 arrived. So, we did it again. Then the

2019 Women's World Cup. Then Euro 2020. And somehow, after all that, we'd raised over £20,000 for some really neat causes, just by not being very good at drawing.

And then we kept going. More bits and bobs of fundraising, a name change to 'No Score Draws', and then, most bafflingly of all, people actually started *buying* our wonky, rubbish drawings, so we've been able to shell out for some nicer pens and pencils and, best of all, an electric pencil sharpener in the shape of a cat to scare our two young children. Wonderful.

Then, one day, a phone call. The conversation that followed began something like this:

'I don't know how to write.'

'Yes, but you don't know how to draw either.'

'Is that Alex and Sian from No Score Draws?'
'It's Alex, yes.'
'From No Score Draws?'
'Yes.'
'The ones who are bad at drawing?'
'Yes, that's us.'
'Excellent. Now, have you ever thought about writing a book?'
'I don't know how to write.'
'Yes, but you don't know how to draw, either.'

It was a good point. The man on the other end of the phone seemed to think that because some poor, misguided folks on Twitter occasionally found our drawings vaguely tolerable, some other people might think so too. What you hold in your hands will put this worryingly shaky theory to the ultimate test. It is the tale of the World Cup, told via the medium of inadequately-drawn faux football stickers. Yes: against our better judgement, under protest, and in spite of everything, they're making us do a book.

Alex and Sian

1930

¡Campeones del mundo!

Host: Uruguay

Winner: Uruguay

It's difficult to believe now, but there was a time before the World Cup. Before the world's best footballers got together for the quadrennial football extravaganza we know and love. Before the goals and the glory, before the iconic kits and the official snack partners, before the dark horses and the surprise packages, before the Golden Boots, the broken metatarsals, the shattered dreams, the vuvuzelas, the cordoned-off fan zones and the flying pints. Before, even, the accompanying sticker album.

A hundred years ago, the fledgling international football scene looked rather different to now. Travel was arduous, and major powers tended to settle disputes not by acquiring sporting bragging rights but by having enormous, costly, terrible wars. Meanwhile if you were British, it was enough to just *assume* you were the superior of every Johnny Foreigner who had the temerity to kick a ball, then rock up to the Olympics every four years to wipe the floor with some Danish amateurs and proclaim yourselves masters of the universe.

With the ascendant Uruguay hoovering up double Olympic football gold in the 1920s, however, the case for some kind of truly global football dust-up gathered pace. Step forward FIFA President Jules Rimet, seen here concealing in his outlandishly roomy head the kernel of an idea that would launch a thousand teary BBC penalty shoot-out montages: the World Cup.

But where to stage it? FIFA quickly settled on Uruguay as host, with the South Americans vowing to build a shiny new stadium as a centrepiece, though

finding teams to play in it would prove somewhat trickier. Despite football's rapid spread around the globe in the early years of the 20th Century, the stark realities of transporting an entire national team's worth of *stuff* (players, kit, smelling salts, Brylcreem, governing body hangers-on, inflatable unicorns etc.) to the other side of the planet for a weeks-long football jolly represented quite an undertaking, and most nations outside the Americas baulked at the cost. At Rimet's urging (and with Uruguay footing the bill for travel expenses), four European teams belatedly entered, with Romania's squad selected by noted football enthusiast King Carol II, depicted overleaf working on some stately tactical innovations (we'll gloss over his flicking hand, last seen attached to John Hurt's face aboard the *Nostromo*). The European teams journeyed together on a single boat, the *SS Conte Verde*, along with Rimet who carried in his bag the trophy Victory, to be awarded to the tournament winners. They were emphatically not joined by Egypt, who missed the boat after being waylaid by a Mediterranean storm. Having never had to draw a boat before, we were helped immeasurably by said vessel having neither eyes nor hands.

Somewhat understandably, it was a tournament of firsts: France's Lucien Laurent bagged the maiden goal and looks justifiably pleased with etching his name into the history books, though the excitement seems to have left him looking a trifle unbalanced. Bert Patenaude of the USA – who may or

An idea that would launch a thousand teary BBC penalty shoot-out montages: the World Cup.

may not be having a reaction to a bee sting – snaffled the first hat-trick, though the 76-year wait for FIFA to finally attribute it to him certainly puts modern VAR delays into perspective. Meanwhile Mexican teenager Manuel Rosas netted the first penalty *and* the first own goal (though unfortunately not at the same time), leaving him with an appropriately perplexed expression.

The Bolivian team paid tribute to their gracious hosts by taking to the pitch against Yugoslavia with 'VIVA URUGUAY' emblazoned on their shirts, a charming gesture which one hopes drew focus from back-to-back 4-0 defeats and the wildly inconsistent length of their shorts. And let's not linger on the chap on the far left who seems to be facing in at least three directions simultaneously. Argentina's Guillermo Stabíle racked up eight goals to claim the inaugural Golden Boot despite looking like a slightly startled Poirot villain, recently discovered in the greenhouse standing over the lifeless body of the Lady of the Manor.

MEXICO 1930

MANUEL ROSAS

BOLIVIA 1930

VIVA URUGUAY

BOLIVIA

ARGENTINA 1930

GUILLERMO STABILE

Guillermo Stabíle racked up eight goals to claim the inaugural Golden Boot despite looking like a slightly startled Poirot villain.

ALBERTO SUPPICI

HÉCTOR CASTRO

The hosts, managed by cricket jumper aficionado Alberto Suppici, triumphed 4-2 over arch-rivals Argentina in the Final, sealed with a last-minute goal from Héctor Castro, sporting the lace-up shirt and alarmingly luscious lips that were typical of the time. Here too is our first primitive attempt at an action shot, featuring some questionable technique (not to mention anatomy) from the Argentine goalkeeper.

URUGUAY 4-2 ARGENTINA

Look, it was 90-odd years ago and we didn't have a lot to go on.

¡CAMPEONES DEL MUNDO!

LUIS MONTI

1934

AZZURI GLORY

Host: Italy

Winner: Italy, obviously

BENITO
MUSSOLINI
1934

EGYPT
1934

In a move sure to have absolutely no future historical parallels, the 1934 World Cup was awarded to Italy under mega-jawed fascist demagogue and sports-washing innovator Benito Mussolini, keen to use the tournament to show off his shiny new totalitarian ideology to the world. Unimpressed by the modest splendour of the Jules Rimet Trophy, Mussolini commissioned his own alternative bearing his name – the Coppa Del Duce – to one would hope near-universal embarrassment. It was massive, ugly, and in no way an over-compensation for anything. Honestly, some dictators.

DAS WUNDERTEAM
1934

After (possibly) waiting on a quayside for four years, Egypt triumphantly marked Africa's entry into the tournament, to be joined by a host of fellow newcomers. Chief among them were the Austrian 'Wunderteam', who combined Viennese coffee house intellectualism with, y'know, being good at kicking a ball and stuff. Their rotating band of attackers were known as the 'Viennese Whirlpool', and were led by Matthias Sindelar,

MATTHIAS
SINDELAR
1934

OLDŘICH
NEJEDLÝ
1934

VITTORIO
POZZO
1934

...aper Man' on account of his
...nd tendency to fall over. To be
...cranium probably didn't help
...problems he may have had.
...y made light of his mismatched
... bottom lip to top the scoring
...choslovakia to a Final date
..., *heavily favoured* hosts. It
... a match too far for the Czechs
...y raincoat connoisseur Vittorio
...ars like the menacing Guiseppe
...dly, the very same Luis Monti
...Argentina in the previous Final),
...xtra time to make off with the
...trophies. Tsk.

GIUSEPPE
MEAZZA
1934

LUIS
MONTI
1934

...AMPIONI DEL MONDO!

1938

FASH FC

Host: France

Winner: Italy, ancora

Much like its predecessor, the 1938 World Cup in France was overshadowed somewhat by the looming spectre of fascism, with scant regard for anyone trying to keep things light when doodling a jokey summary 80-odd years later. With Europe on the cusp of war and ideological clashes (the non-fun geopolitical kind, not the tiki-taka versus long-ball kind) at every turn, the tournament took place in something of a powder-keg atmosphere.

After both nations had already qualified, Nazi Germany annexed neighbouring Austria and fielded a combined team where one would suspect everyone got on absolutely famously. Really, can't believe we've had to draw a swastika, but that *was* their flag and we are absolute sticklers for accuracy in all matters that don't involve drawing human faces.

Reigning champs Italy endeared themselves to the French crowds with straight-armed salutes before each game, then when drawn against the hosts in the quarter-finals opted to wear ever-so-slightly provocative black shirts for *the only time in their history*. Subtle this was not, the significance not lost on our perturbed smudge of a referee.

In desperate search of some levity for this chapter we tried to draw three Swedish lads having a cuddle, only for it to inadvertently turn into some kind of nightmarish many-headed hydra type thing from *Resident Evil*.

Let's move on to pencil-'tached Brazilian Leônidas, seen here reacting in real time to our attempts to draw him, who bagged the Golden Boot. Please note the extraordinary restraint we've shown in making no reference to his Spartan namesake. It would have been very easy to depict him stylishly booting an unsuspecting centre-half into a big pit, but we're better than that. Possibly.

While regrettably very much in the pocket of Big Fash, Italy were undeniably still a heck of a team, and inspired by the goals of rictus-grinned marionette Silvio Piola they eased to victory over Hungary in the Final to retain their title.

Coach Vittorio Pozzo, by now apparently almost fully transformed into a friendly vampire count, remains the only man to coach two World Cup-winning sides.

1950

THE CUP WITHOUT A FINAL

Host: Brazil

Winner: ~~Brazil~~ Uruguay

ENGLAND 1950

STANLEY MATTHEWS

ENGLAND 1950

OH, ENGLAND

UNITED STATES 1950

JOE GAETJENS

With most of the world preoccupied with post-war rebuilding, FIFA bit Brazil's hand off when the South Americans offered to host the World Cup's belated fourth edition. England finally deigned to attend, and prepared in the time-honoured style by, er, sending their star winger Stanley Matthews on a promotional tour of Canada. There he is considering a Mountie. This was our first time drawing a horse, but hours of diligent research led us to believe they look more or less like this. We're genuinely quite proud of it. Might just stick to horses from now on.

Having spent a week or so acclimatising and making friends by complaining about the heat, accommodation and food, England set about stinking the place out. A laboured win over Chile was followed by an unthinkable, cataclysmic and remarkably funny defeat to the ragtag amateurs of the USA, represented by an assortment of dishwashers, postmen, hearse drivers and, most damningly of all, ex-Wrexham wing-halves. Haitian immigrant Joe Gaetjens scored the winning goal, with some sources suggesting a speculative longshot hit him square in the face on the way to

SPAIN 1950

ZARRA

BRAZIL 1950

ADEMIR

BRAZIL 1950

MOACIR BARBOSA

wrong-footing goalkeeper Bert Williams, which would go some way to explaining Joe's expression here. Drawing faces is hard, you know? A goal from the frighteningly grumpy Zarra ensured another meek defeat against Spain and England were massively out, vowing never again to arrive at a World Cup with a misplaced air of optimism.

URUGUAY 1950
ALCIDES GHIGGIA

Meanwhile in other hubris news the hosts, buoyed by the gigantic crowds of the cavernous Maracanã and the gigantic neck of centre forward Ademir, were busily scoring stupid amounts of goals as the tournament entered the business end. By the time of the decider against Uruguay in front of 200,000 souls, Brazil had walloped 23 goals past various startled defences and started as overwhelming favourites, with newspaper headlines already proclaiming them champions and a pitch-side band ready to launch into a specially written samba to celebrate their *inevitable* victory. Hopefully the assembled musicians were at least able to provide a soundtrack of comedy parp-parp noises as Uruguay's rakish Alcides Ghiggia raced away to score the winning goal, plunging the Maracanã into mourning and Brazilian keeper Moacir Barbosa into an existential funk. The defeated Brazilians collapsed to the turf in dismay and not, as we appear to have depicted, in an impromptu display of interpretive dance. The defeat, an epochal humiliation in front of their own fans, would go down in history as the *Maracanãço*. Still, at least it was only 2-1...

THE MARACANAÇO
BRAZIL
1950

The defeated Brazilians collapsed to the turf in dismay and not, as we appear to have depicted, in an impromptu display of interpretive dance.

CAMPEONES DEL MUNDO!
URUGUAY
1950

1954

FUSSBALL-WELTMEISTERSCHAFT

Host: Switzerland

Winner: West Germany

THE GOLDEN TEAM

The World Cup boomeranged back to Europe in 1954, with Switzerland providing the backdrop for a tournament featuring lots of weather, a slightly daft number of goals and a competition format of truly Patridgean convolutedness. The Hungarians' famed 'Golden Team' were the heavy favourites, boasting a galaxy of stars fresh from banjaxing England 6-3 at

Wembley the previous year with their tactical subtleties and unsettling boggle-eyed stares. Deep-lying centre-forward Nándor Hidegkuti (one eye making a break for it) created space for the likes of Sándor Kocsis (possible nervous twitch) and Ferenc 'Oh Lawd He Comin'' Puskás, with the team unbeaten in three years heading into the tournament.

NÁNDOR HIDEGKUTI

SÁNDOR KOCSIS

FERENC PUSKÁS

The Hungarians' famed 'Golden Team' were the heavy favourites, boasting a galaxy of stars fresh from banjaxing England 6-3 at Wembley the previous year.

LUIGI FRANCO GEMMA 1954

JOHNNY MACKENZIE 1954

Turkey made their World Cup bow having seen off Spain in the qualifiers via the mystifyingly discontinued method of drawing with each other and then asking a blindfolded Italian youth to pick a winner. Modern World Cups really don't have enough of this sort of thing.

Meanwhile Scotland (after sulkily sitting out in 1950 in a baffling display of self-martyrdom having failed to win the Home International Championships) finally made their World Cup debut in a blaze of predictable calamity. Name a 22-man squad to fully allow for any and all eventualities? Nah, 13 will do. Blithely assume alpine

Switzerland is freezing all year round and pack a load of inch-thick woolly shirts? Absolutely. Pad out your travelling party with endless blazered men and their wives? Don't mind if we do. Crush your new manager's spirits so thoroughly he resigns after the first game? Why not! Johnny Mackenzie sums up the Scots' travails, a frazzled husk sweating away under the baking Zurich sun. Scotland lost both games, conceded eight times and went home without scoring a goal. Onwards and upwards though, eh?

The quarter-finals were an awful lot of fun. The '**Battle of Berne**' saw Hungary and Brazil spend 90 minutes hoofing lumps out of

JÓZSEF BOZSIK 1954

NILTON SANTOS 1954

HEAT BATTLE OF LAUSANNE

FRITZ WALTER

HELMUT RAHN

each other in a textbook example of Scenes That No One Wants To See, the match descending into a running battle that continued long after the final whistle. Hopefully our depiction of József Bozsik and Nilton Santos exchanging gentle neck massages adequately conveys the sheer unrelenting violence of the occasion. On the other side of the draw, the '**Heat Battle of Lausanne**' saw the hosts and Austria collectively decide that 40°C weather was simply far too hot to bother with defending, the Austrians shrugging off an early 3-0 deficit (which owed, one would think, rather a lot to their 'keeper having actual heatstroke) to record a pleasingly Sunday League-ish 7-5 win. All very silly.

The Final saw the Hungarians leap swiftly into a 2-0 lead against the underdog West Germans and, having already given them an 8-3 pasting in the group stage, seemed set fair for victory. But the Germans roared back, boosted by the heavy rain and *allegedly* quite a lot of amphetamines, and inspired by asymmetrical skipper Fritz Walter, whose prowess in the wet led the West Germans to dub such downpours 'Fritz Walter Weather' in a dizzying display of imagination. Helmut Rahn ignored his mismatched ears to nab the winning goals, sealing '**The Miracle of Bern**' and – at least in our depiction – leading to a pitch invasion by fans who may or may not have first helped themselves to some *refreshments* from the West German dressing room.

DIE WELTMEISTER!

1958

THE PELÉ SHOW

Host: Sweden

Winner: Braziiiiilllll

TOM FINNEY

BILLY WRIGHT

LEV YASHIN

Sweden were the hosts in 1958 where, for the first and only time at a World Cup (parochialism alert) all four of Britain's home nations qualified, happily meaning plenty of hard-luck stories for us to mine for this silly book. Scotland (already warming to their theme) duly bowed out in the first-round, as did England who, reeling from the tragic losses of the Munich air disaster, fielded a callow squad held together by septuagenarian duo Tom Finney and Billy Wright. Our drawing of dear Billy is difficult to explain, but we've got a fairly new baby and aren't getting enough sleep so let's blame it on that. Legendary Soviet 'keeper Lev Yashin's cat-like agility (and one apparently very small leg) was enough to see off England, who for the third straight tournament departed without making much of a dent.

Debutants Northern Ireland shocked the world by knocking out Italy in qualifying, drawing with West Germany and then dispatching the fancied Czechs with a brace from the terrifyingly smiley Peter McParland. Goalkeeper Harry Gregg, a hero

PETER McPARLAND

HARRY GREGG

JUST
FONTAINE

IVOR
ALLCHURCH

PELÉ

of Munich just months previously, starred throughout their run to the quarter-finals, where unfortunately they ran into France. And France meant Just Fontaine, who spent the World Cup scoring a scarcely credible thirteen goals in six games, the kind of impossible immersion-breaking statistic that would fatally undermine any right-thinking person's Football Manager save.

Forgive our petty tribal excitement, but WALES made a fine fist of their first and (until their inevitable, dominant triumph in Qatar 2022) only time at a World Cup, illuminating the tournament by, er, failing to win any of their group games. No, they were actually a lot better than that sounds, beating a creaking Hungary in a playoff via an incredible goal from handsome devil Ivor Allchurch and earning a quarter-final with... ah, Brazil, and a 17-year-old Santos prodigy by the name of Pelé.

Don't let our sunken-eyed portrait fool you – Pelé arrived at his first World Cup a bundle of youthful ball-juggling effervescence, it's just we just haven't been able to capture any of that here. After callously crushing the hopes and dreams of

KURT
HAMRIN

Skew-whiff syllable-hoarders Didi and Vavá.

WALES like some kind of monster, he outgunned Fontaine with a semi-final hat-trick to book a Final place against the hosts, whose path through the tournament had been built on comparatively workmanlike performances and the goals of flailing ninny Kurt Hamrin. The Final saw Pelé announce himself to the world as football's first truly global superstar as – aided by the artistry of skew-whiff syllable-hoarders Didi and Vavá – he led Sweden a merry dance, scoring twice in a thrilling 5-2 win. Sadly, this drawing was the best we could do in trying to convey Pelé's otherworldly prowess. Yes, he was genuinely capable of kicking a ball in the air a bit and a whole lot more, we promise, it's just we're working from a very limited toolbox here.

1962

GARRINCHACHACHA

Host: Chile

Winner:
This could become a theme

Chile. 1962. The BBC's David Coleman, introducing highlights of hosts Chile's clash with Italy, stares solemnly down the camera lens, face like thunder, the full disapproving weight of authority at his back, and gravely intones the words: 'Good evening. The game you are about to see is the most stupid, appalling, disgusting and disgraceful exhibition of football, possibly in the history of the game.' Whether or not poor, scandalised David was aware that the average viewer's anticipation levels were trebling with his every grumpy adjective is a moot point, but there's no doubt he neatly summed up the overarching vibe of the World Cup's return to South America, which was: what if football, but insane?

The '**Battle of Santiago**' as it became known *while it was still happening* has gone down as the most violent World Cup match in history, and with excellent reason. The first foul took less than twelve seconds, the first sending-off less than eight minutes, at which point the sheer density of the descending red mist makes things a little hazy. What is certain is that haymakers were thrown, the local (armed) constabulary repeatedly intervened to drag offenders from the field of play, there was spitting, elbowing, ludicrous neck-high lunging, and at the centre of it all an understandably frazzled and inevitably English referee trying gamely to prevent a major diplomatic incident. That man in the middle, Ken Aston, would go on to invent yellow and red cards, charmingly believing that some pieces of coloured cardboard would succeed where actual men with guns had failed.

THE BATTLE OF SANTIAGO

The first foul took less than twelve seconds, the first sending-off less than eight minutes, at which point the sheer density of the descending red mist makes things a little hazy.

KEN ASTON

In illustrating such carnage, we toyed with the idea of the classic 'big ball of dust with arms and legs poking out' but, in order to accurately convey the sheer barbarity, it seemed a montage of poses cribbed from *Mortal Kombat II* would be better. Also of note: this was one of several attempts we made at drawing dear David Coleman, and it is to our eternal shame that this was the best one. Sometimes you just have to admit defeat and move on.

DAVID COLEMAN

CHILE v ITALY

ENGLAND 1-3 BRAZIL

Sometimes you just have to admit defeat and move on.

In a tournament permeated by a raging battle fever that was by no means restricted to Chile's and Italy's notorious throwdown, it was fortunate that England were there to provide some levity. Drawn against champs and favourites Brazil in the quarter-finals, England were given the runaround first by the diminutive, bandy-legged Garrincha,

JIMMY GREAVES

GARRINCHA & 'BI'

and then by the diminutive, bandy-legged dog who scampered onto the field of play, halting the game for some minutes. After evading several challenges with some nifty paw-work (just go with it), the canine interloper was finally apprehended by England's Jimmy Greaves, whose reward was an invigorating stream of piping hot dog wee down the front of his jersey. Once again, we find ourselves bemoaning Stuff Like This not happening enough at World Cups anymore. The offending hound was subsequently adopted by the Brazilian squad and raffled, with Garrincha himself taking the lucky pup (newly rechristened 'Bi') home with him, as seen in our affecting illustration of the happy couple. A heart-warming conclusion, though one wonders as to Bi's fate if he'd invaded the pitch during the Chile versus Italy game.

Amidst a gaggle of players to share the Golden Boot, we simply couldn't *not* draw Valentin Ivanov, who bagged four goals for the USSR and dazzled opposing defences with some of the most powerful eyebrows to ever grace a World Cup.

Valentin Ivanov bagged four goals for the USSR and dazzled opposing defences with some of the most powerful eyebrows to ever grace a World Cup.

VALENTIN IVANOV

AMARILDO

VAVÁ

Having befriended and communed with the raw power of the animal kingdom, and despite being Pelé-less for much of the tournament, Brazil proceeded serenely to the Final where they retained the cup with a 3-1 win over Czechoslovakia. Pelé's utterly furious-looking deputy Amarildo showed the way before Vavá, who we've been forced to draw for the second time in this book to no discernible improvement, became the first man to score in two World Cup Finals. Captain Mauro Ramos lifted the trophy high, apparently above a couple of men with large quiffs. We've done our research so this absolutely must have happened.

We've done our research so this absolutely must have happened.

CAMPEÕES DA COPA DO MUNDO!

1966

THE YEAR IT CAME HOME

Host: England

Winner: England,
which is honestly fine

Full disclosure: despite living there and drinking deeply from the fetid well of its football culture, we're not English. So, before we semi-grudgingly get to the bit where Alf Ramsey's England (spoiler alert) win the cursed thing, let's deal with the other, more fun bits of the 1966 World Cup. First up: LARCENY! The Jules Rimet Trophy itself was stolen from a London exhibition in the runup to the tournament, before being found under a hedge by a dog, a dog we are duty bound by our publishing agreement to draw, meaning this book – this book about football – now contains a statistically improbable number of drawings of dogs. How did it come to this?

Just as surprising as this tome's dogs-to-footballers ratio was the impact made by the tournament's debutants. North Korea's fledgling team, who'd only played their first official game two years previously and were so politically isolated that FIFA and the FA did away with national anthems for the majority of the tournament rather than give theirs

airtime, went and beat two-time champions Italy in one of the biggest shocks in football history. Pak Doo-Ik and his fabulous cheekbones netted the winner, earning the North Koreans an unlikely quarter-final place and Italy a date with approximately 6,000 rotten tomatoes on their return home. Depicting this harrowing scene, these elite

athletes being pelted with rancid produce, was a challenge we embraced the only way we know how: with cheap felt tip pens and a lingering sense of our own shortcomings.

Fellow newcomers Portugal also made a splash, with Eusébio – who unfortunately looks here like his jaw is trying to escape from his face – scoring goals for fun as they dumped favourites Brazil out in the group stage. Pity poor Pelé, who spent the tournament being booted up in the air under leaden Merseyside skies, departing the Goodison Park pitch wrapped in an overcoat in what we've just realised was an unerring foreshadowing of the climactic scenes of *Escape to Victory*. Weird.

Eusébio – who unfortunately looks here like his jaw is trying to escape from his face

BOBBY CHARLTON

ANTONIO RATTÍN

GEOFF HURST

JACK CHARLTON

Okay, fine, let's do England. They stodged their way to an early stalemate with Uruguay, before a rocket from the defiantly becombovered Bobby Charlton against Mexico ignited their group stage charge. A win over France saw them safely through to a somewhat feisty quarter-final with Argentina, whose captain Antonio Rattín is pictured here accepting his early sending off with admirable sangfroid. Unheralded backup striker Geoff Hurst, in for the luckless (though, this time, mercifully unsoiled) Jimmy Greaves, stepped up to score the winner, before a combination of Bobby Charlton's feet and his brother Jack's hands saw off Portugal in the semis. And just like that, manager Alf Ramsey's 'wingless wonders' were in the Final.

Antonio Rattín is pictured here accepting his early sending off with admirable sangfroid.

ALF RAMSEY

HELMUT HALLER

MARTIN PETERS

GEOFF HURST

BONK

HANS TILKOWSKI

TOFIQ BAHRAMOV

Their opponents would be West Germany. An early goal from Helmut Haller, pictured here doing a really hard sum in his head, was swiftly cancelled out by Hurst, before a late strike from his blisteringly unflatteringly drawn clubmate Martin Peters looked to have sealed victory. With time ticking away though, Wolfgang Weber poked home a last-gasp equaliser, because nothing in life is ever easy, least of all drawing footballers.

Extra-time, then. Ramsey famously told his charges 'You've won it once. Now you'll have to go out there and win it again,' which, though technically untrue, was, fair's fair, a decent line. As the clock ticked past 100 minutes, Hurst – unperturbed by apparently having castanets for hands – turned and shot against the bar, the ball fizzing down and bouncing somewhere in the vicinity of the goal-line, then up and away. Amidst the bedlam, Azeri linesman Tofiq Bahramov confirmed the ball had absolutely, definitively and with cast-iron certainty *probably* crossed the line, and the goal was duly given.

(Bahramov's contribution to football history is honoured by having the Azeri national stadium named in his honour, plus a big statue of himself, and yet the Premier League still refuses to erect a thousand-foot-tall golden effigy of Mike Dean at Stockwell Park. Pathetic, really.)

With seconds remaining, England broke up field one final time. Time stood still. Planets formed and died. As Hurst streaked clear of the West German defence, the over-eager crowd already spilling onto the field, BBC commentator Kenneth Wolstenholme sniffed immortality. 'Some people are on the pitch... they think it's all over...' he intoned, moments before Hurst ~~sensibly took the ball to the corner flag~~ hammered an unstoppable shot high into Hans Tilkowski's net. 'It is now!' concluded our Ken, possibly before throwing down his mic and knee-sliding out of the commentary box.

"THEY THINK IT'S ALL OVER..."

"IT IS NOW!"

'It is now!' concluded our Ken, possibly before throwing down his mic and knee-sliding out of the commentary box.

#NICETOUCH

NOBBY STILES

The scenes that followed are so well-known that they almost survive our attempts to reproduce them. Skipper Bobby Moore wiping his mucky hands on the velvet of the Royal Box to avoid sullying the Queen's gloves, a move that if enacted now would elicit enough handclap emojis to tilt the earth off its axis. The jigging Nobby Stiles and his friendly/terrifying (delete as applicable) grin. And Moore, aloft on his team-mates' shoulders, Jules Rimet newly gleaming, almost certainly ushering in decades of English World Cup domination, the 'Years of Hurt' counter reset to zero.

YEARS OF HURT: 0

1970

THE BRAZIL SHOW

Host: Mexico

Winner: Brazil. Yes, them again

BRAZIL
1970
PELÉ
v ENGLAND

ENGLAND
1970
BOBBY
MOORE

T he Mexico World Cup of 1970 was
(let's face it) all about Brazil, with
the advent of colour TV and crackling
transatlantic phone commentary arriving
just in time to imprint the dazzling yellows
and blues of their sublime attacking play all
over the collective football memory.

Their first-round clash with defending
champions England was a classic, with
'keeper Gordon Banks' lumpen, rudimentary
hand denying Pelé with the 'Save of the
Century', before Bobby Moore shrugged
off a spurious pre-tournament run-in with
South American law enforcement to execute
one of the greatest tackles of all time on
a flying Jairzinho. We don't know if books
have any kind of age restriction/rating, but
if this one does it will likely be down to our
depiction of Bobby's shorts. Jairzinho and
his imperceptibly raised eyebrow would
ultimately settle the game, but the lasting

**Bobby Moore shrugged
off a spurious pre-
tournament run-in with
South American law
enforcement to execute
one of the greatest
tackles of all time on a
flying Jairzinho.**

BRAZIL
1970
JAIRZINHO

image would be the post-match embrace between Pelé and Moore, speaking of a deep mutual respect criminally undermined by our attempts to draw it.

England proceeded to a quarter-final meeting with West Germany, their preparations hampered by goalkeeper Banks' untimely difficulties in the digestive tract department. His deputy Peter Bonetti – actually a handsome man in real life who we have absolutely failed to do justice – wilted under the harsh glare, as England stuffed up a 2-0 lead to fall victim to a late winner from Gerd Müller and his vacant yet piercing stare.

The post-match embrace between Pelé and Moore, speaking of a deep mutual respect criminally undermined by our attempts to draw it.

Pelé meanwhile was having the time of his life playing in a World Cup while not being hoofed from pillar to post, and spent most of the tournament trying to score increasingly preposterous goals, detailed here in a selection of clumsy scrawls. First off, he tried his luck from his own half against Czechoslovakia with the kind of opportunistic 60-yard punt that was as thrillingly unlikely fifty years ago as it is mundanely passé now every Sunday league game is filmed on an iPhone, followed by an ostentatious dummy against Uruguay that left goalkeeper Ladislao Mazurkiewicz several timezones east of Guadalajara. It's fair to say

that the levels of anatomical correctness displayed in these renderings are plumbing new depths, so for that we apologise.

Brazil sashayed to the Final to face Italy, who'd come through an enthralling semi-final with West Germany later dubbed the '**Game of the Century**' (with appalling disregard for Wales' 3-1 win over Belgium at Euro 2016), the defining image of which was the West Germans' Franz Beckenbauer dragging himself through extra-time with his shoulder held together by goodwill and sticky tape. Inspired by the goals of the fearsomely chiselled Gigi Riva, Italy presented Brazil's biggest challenge yet.

And Brazil *walloped* them. Their fourth goal was their finest hour, their crowning glory, and absolutely not something that we are in any way capable of adequately depicting here. We'll settle for some constituent parts – Clodoaldo wading through a morass of knackered Italians, Jairzinho's first touch as he killed Rivellino's pass down the line, Toastão – his outsized, misshapen dome baking under the Azteca sun – pointing where to play the ball, Pelé tenderly rolling it into the path of the onrushing Carlos Alberto, the skipper arriving from out of shot to crash home, both feet off the floor, the greatest goal of all time.*

*Apart from Hal Robson-Kanu's.

Their fourth goal was their finest hour, their crowning glory, and absolutely not something that we are in any way capable of adequately depicting here.

1974

Total Football

Host: West Germany

Winner: Jawohl

JAN
JONGBLOED WM 74

JOHAN
CRUYFF WM 74

First things first: the Netherlands did not win the 1974 World Cup in West Germany. Another, different team won it, but we'll get to that bit. Because though they didn't win it, the Netherlands had an abundance of what has come to be known as Main Character Energy. They were unquestionably the *protagonists*. They looked cool. They had fabulous hair and lovely big sideburns. Their playing style was not only unique, well-defined and brilliantly effective but also had a really neat name: *Total Football*. They doled out their squad numbers alphabetically, so their goalkeeper wore number 8. Number 8! Their beautiful orange Adidas shirts were, in the words of an imaginary identikit young person we've just conjured, absolutely sick. We are very old.

And then there was their talisman Johan Cruyff, who in a team bursting with style and personality managed to still stand apart. Where his teammates' shirts had three Adidas stripes, his personal sponsorship deal with Puma meant his had just two. Where his teammates' numbers were alphabetical, he wore his favoured #14. In a Main Character Energy team, he was the Main Character. Just ignore the oversize tongue we've furnished him with.

The *Oranje* cut a swathe through the tournament, besting Uruguay, hammering Argentina, outclassing Brazil. The abiding image though came from their group game with Sweden, when Cruyff introduced the world to his masterpiece, his magnum opus, his 180 degrees of sass: the Cruyff turn,

Their playing style was not only unique, well-defined and brilliantly effective but also had a really neat name: *Total Football*.

sending poor Jan Olsson for the ultimate hotdog which, regrettably, we have chosen to illustrate with a punishing literalness. And yes, those are the correct floodlights of the Westfalenstadion in 1974. Do not doubt us.

(Honesty time: after drawing this nonsense, a crisis of confidence ensued when we started worrying about awareness levels of the phrase 'sent for a hotdog.' Some in-depth research (and absolutely not a brief Twitter poll) led us to believe that approximately 60 per cent of readers will understand the phrase. To the remaining 40 per cent, we can only apologise.)

Elsewhere, debutants Zaire provided one of the most iconic, if misunderstood moments,

in World Cup history during their match with Brazil. Already 2-0 down and facing a dangerous free-kick, Zaire's Mwepu Ilunga suddenly sprinted headlong out of the defensive wall and punted the dead ball miles downfield. As Ilunga was booked for his troubles amid widespread mirth and bemusement, commentator John Motson depressingly assumed 'a bizarre moment of African ignorance' as if Ilunga, *who was playing at an actual World Cup* remember, didn't know the flipping rules. The reality was more than a little different: heavy defeat in their previous game with Yugoslavia had left their players fearing pariah status (or worse)

ZAIRE v BRAZIL · WM 74

ZAIRE v BRAZIL · WM 74

MWEPU ILUNGA · WM 74

on their return to their homeland, which cowered under the cartoonishly evil President Mobutu's iron fist. Fearing the consequences of a further drubbing, Ilunga was simply trying to waste a bit of time to keep the score down. Can't say we blame him.

A late goal from dentistry's Joe Jordan against Yugoslavia saw Scotland flirt dangerously with avoiding a first-round exit, though thankfully for desperate writer/doodlers looking for unsubtle narrative through-lines for substandard books everywhere, they didn't quite manage it. Meanwhile Poland's bedraggled Grzegorz Lato nabbed the Golden Boot, striking a valuable blow against the numerous magnificent heads of hair that dominated the tournament.

JOE JORDAN · WM 74

GRZEGORZ LATO · WM 74

JOHAN NEESKENS — WM 74

PAUL BREITNER — WM 74

GERD MÜLLER — WM 74

The Final was a juicy affair, pitting the masterly Dutch against the hosts and reigning European Champions West Germany, perhaps the only team in the tournament who could match them for both talent *and* facial hair. Johan Neeskens and his luxurious mutton chops converted an early penalty, swiftly cancelled out by Paul Breitner, before '*Der Bomber*' Gerd Müller swivelled his chonkily-drawn frame to fire home what proved to be the winner. For all their brilliance and beauty, the Dutch were beaten, with Cruyff later wondering aloud whether they had in fact been the real winners, thus showing it was he who had a surprising misunderstanding of the rules of Association Football. Is that goalkeeper Sepp Maier kissing the shiny new World Cup, or is he receiving from Franz Beckenbauer a playful trophy-boop on the nose? We may never know.

DIE WELTMEISTER! — WM 74

Is that goalkeeper Sepp Maier receiving from Franz Beckenbauer a playful trophy-boop on the nose? We may never know.

1978

Don't Cry For Me

Host: Argentina

Winner: Argentina, obviamente

ARGENTINA 78

JORGE RAFAEL VIDELA

ARGENTINA 78

9P

SCOTLAND

With a weary sigh, we come to yet another World Cup played in a country run by scumbags. Boooo. Argentina's ruling military junta meant a 1978 edition that was heavy on admittedly very cool tickertape but light on good vibes, played against a backdrop of 'dirty war', jailed dissidents and allegations of skulduggery and corruption that endure to this day. Fun!

Fortunately, Scotland were on hand to lighten the mood with everybody's favourite World Cup ingredient: HUBRIS. Buoyed by the proclamations of manager/hype-man Ally MacLeod and sent on their way by thousands of well-wishers, expectations were *high*. While a little confidence is no bad thing, (and Scotland after all had several world class players, plus a favourable draw against the likes of Iran and Peru) the decision to have commemorative postage stamps already designed to celebrate their

forthcoming victory *may* have tweaked the nose of fate just a little too hard.

And so it was that after a *lot* of big talk, MacLeod found himself at half-time of their opener against Peru telling goalkeeper Alan Rough to kick the ball harder to clear their opponents' dominant midfield. Delicious. Here's poor Alan, straining every sinew, bless him. A pair of outrageous longshots

ARGENTINA 78

ALAN ROUGH

ARGENTINA 78

TEÓFILO CUBILLAS

ARGENTINA 78

ALLY MACLEOD

from Teófilo Cubillas (including a glorious outside-of-the-boot free-kick past a grotesquely malformed defensive wall) consigned the Scots to defeat, before an abject draw with Iran left MacLeod with his head in his misshapen, claw-like hands. Only a massively unlikely three-goal win over the fancied Dutch would save the Scots. They couldn't, could they? Well, no. Despite a belatedly brilliant performance and an incredible solo goal from Archie Gemmill (whom we owe an enormous apology for whatever this drawing is), their 3-2 victory just wasn't enough. Without the suffocating pressure of expectation, who knows what could have been? We blame the stamps.

Archie Gemmill (whom we owe an enormous apology for whatever this drawing is)

ARGENTINA 78

ARCHIE GEMMILL

ARGENTINA 78
HANS KRANKL

ARGENTINA 78
ROB RENSENBRINK

Away from Scotland's travails, it was a tournament of deeply handsome men whose lustre we have absolutely failed to do justice: the hunched beauty of Austria's Hans Krankl, the undead allure of the Netherlands' Rob Rensenbrink, the appropriately explosive hair of Roberto Dinamite, the gunslinger's poise of Leopoldo 'Lucky' Luque. We've drawn them all, and they all look like they wish we hadn't.

ARGENTINA 78
ROBERTO DINAMITE

ARGENTINA 78
LEOPOLDO LUQUE

Away from Scotland's travails, it was a tournament of deeply handsome men whose lustre we have absolutely failed to do justice.

Meanwhile, and without wanting to draw too much attention to our nationality, we've spotted a chance to shoehorn some WALES content in here and we're going to take it. Presenting: Clive Thomas, gleefully officious maverick referee of Brazil's opener with Sweden. With the game delicately poised at one-all and Brazil's Nelinho stood over a last-gasp corner kick, Thomas noticed as the kick was taken that a whopping *six seconds* of injury time had already elapsed. Too much for our Clive, who blew his whistle just as Zico headed in what would have been the winning goal. Letting a team take a corner, but not score from it: truly, the kind of pedantry that

Argentina went on to defeat the Dutch after extra-time thanks to two goals from Timotei addict Mario Kempes.

ARGENTINA 78

CÉSAR LUIS MENOTTI

ARGENTINA 78

MARIO KEMPES

has ensured universal, undying admiration for men in black across the globe. You've got to respect that. Just don't peer too closely at our fun-house mirror drawing of him. With a Cruyff-less but still dangerous Netherlands awaiting in the Final, the tournament's convoluted structure ultimately meant the hosts, under the tutelage of helmet-haired chain-smoker César Luis Menotti, needed at least a four-goal victory over the hitherto impressive Peru to squeeze through. Amid rumours of conveniently unfrozen Peruvian assets, unsolicited grain deliveries and dressing room visits by junta bigwigs, Argentina stormed to a *remarkably unlikely* 6-0 win. Hmmmm. Reprieved by this *wildly unexpected* hammering, Argentina went on to defeat the Dutch after extra-time thanks to two goals from Timotei addict Mario Kempes, with grinning smudge Daniel Passarella lifting the trophy over a sea of spent tickertape.

ARGENTINA 78

¡CAMPEONES DEL MUNDO!

1982

¡Ole Ol-ouch!

Host: Spain

Winner: Italia

ESPAÑA 82

DAVID
NAREY
SCOTLAND

ESPAÑA 82

ALAN
ROUGH
SCOTLAND

ESPAÑA 82

ALAN HANSEN &
WILLIE MILLER
SCOTLAND

Spain were the hosts for the enlarged 1982 tournament, with a whopping twenty-four teams meaning a truly upsetting number of inadequate drawings from us, so strap in. We'll start with the inevitable: Scotland's customary humiliation. This time it involved angering Brazil with an early David Narey goal to provoke a majestic 4-1 thrashing (highlighted by Alan Rough becoming the most thoroughly lobbed goalkeeper in football history), before the slapstick comedy stylings of Alan Hansen and Willie Miller against the USSR completed their pratfall to an inexorable first round exit. Exemplary. England meanwhile arrived with a lovely kit, didn't lose any games despite playing France, Spain and West Germany, then went home. Sometimes life isn't fair, the enormity of the injustice matched only by Kevin Keegan's expansive barnet.

ESPAÑA 82

KEVIN
KEEGAN
ENGLAND

Sometimes life isn't fair, the enormity of the injustice matched only by Kevin Keegan's expansive barnet.

ESPAÑA 82

GERRY ARMSTRONG
NORTHERN IRELAND

ESPAÑA 82

NORMAN WHITESIDE
NORTHERN IRELAND

ESPAÑA 82

SALAH ASSAD
ALGERIA

ESPAÑA 82

GRÉGOIRE M'BIDA
CAMEROON

ESPAÑA 82

LÁSZLÓ KISS
HUNGARY

A host of unfancied teams made their mark. The dourly moustachioed Gerry Armstrong and the frightening man-child physique of 17-year-old prodigy Norman Whiteside combined to give Northern Ireland a shock win over the hosts, the worryingly gaunt Salah Assad earned debutants Algeria victory over West Germany, while the handsomely fretful Grégoire M'Bida starred for unbeaten Cameroon in their draw with Italy. Things were less fun for Honduras, whose record 10-1 battering by Hungary required some hasty mid-match scoreboard maintenance, the fittingly pouty substitute László Kiss helping himself to a record eight-minute hat-trick.

ESPAÑA 82

HUNGARY 1 0
EL SALVADOR 1

EL SALVADOR 1
HUNGARY 10

Argentine prodigy Diego Maradona made his World Cup bow amidst much fuss and attention, not least from some overly physical opponents. Pummelled this way and that throughout, things reached an apogee with the crude bodily harm meted out by Italian hatchet-man Claudio Gentile, who spent the entirety of their second-round clash finding new and ingenious ways of booting Maradona into the Barcelona sky. Look at poor Diego, kicked so hard he can scarcely maintain human form.

Elsewhere, Kuwait's game with France was interrupted by the tiny Gulf nation's Sheikh Fahad, who stomped onto the field of play to remonstrate with the referee,

Look at poor Diego, kicked so hard he can scarcely maintain human form.

successfully lobbying to have a French goal chalked off after Kuwait's players apparently heard a whistle from the crowd. How best to illustrate an overturned refereeing decision from the early 1980s? We present to you: the Betamax Assistant Referee. We struggled a bit with this one, we're not going to lie.

And then there was Brazil. Their class of '82 were possibly the most easy-on-the-eye team to ever grace a World Cup, a claim we accept isn't supported by these upsetting daubings of Sócrates and Éder. With the peerless (though horribly sweaty) Zico pulling the strings, they sauntered through their group while scoring a host of comically brilliant goals. Tragically, though, for fair-weather aesthetes everywhere, they also viewed defending as some sort of optional extra which they could probably get by without, and duly came a cropper in an all-time classic against a Paolo Rossi-inspired Italy. Rossi, shown here looking almost,

but not quite, entirely unlike himself, was newly returned from a two-year match-fixing ban, and put his understandably fresh legs to good use to snaffle a hat-trick and send Brazil home, before scoring twice more against Poland to book Italy's place in the Final.

Their opponents West Germany were not the easiest bunch to warm to. Their group stage had seen them contrive a mutually beneficial draw with Austria in what became known as the '**Disgrace of Gijón**', the two teams dawdling for eighty-odd quarter-paced minutes to universal fury, safe in the knowledge their cosy 1-1 draw would eliminate luckless Algeria instead. Difficult to sum up in one poorly drawn football

ESPAÑA 82

ZBIGNIEW
BONIEK
POLAND

ESPAÑA 82

KARL-HEINZ
RUMMENIGGE
WEST GERMANY

ESPAÑA 82

THE DISGRACE
OF GIJÓN
WEST GERMANY V AUSTRIA

sticker, you'd have thought. And you'd be right. They followed up this travesty with the '**Night of Seville**', a pulsating semi-final with France featuring the highest of high drama, six goals and almost as many lost teeth. With the game level at the hour mark, French substitute Patrick Battiston chased a bouncing ball into the West German box, whereupon 'keeper Harald 'Toni' Schumacher came thundering out of his goal, leapt through the air and *arsed* poor

Difficult to sum up in one poorly drawn football sticker, you'd have thought. And you'd be right.

TONI SCHUMACHER
WEST GERMANY

THE NIGHT OF SEVILLE

PATRICK BATTISTON
FRANCE

Battiston all the way back to Saint-Étienne. With his unconscious victim left twitching on the turf, the mystifyingly unpunished Schumacher stood impassively, hands on hips, waiting to take the resultant goal kick, then compounded a bravura display of supervillainy by saving two spot-kicks to win the first ever World Cup penalty shoot-out. Ouch.

Thankfully for fans of instant karmic justice it was the Italians who triumphed in the Final, a match best remembered for Marco Tardelli's majestically tiny-shorted, sweat-sodden and berserkly operatic goal celebration. Our chasm-mouthed portrayal of Tardelli's moment isn't something we're particularly proud of, though it certainly beats our attempts at the post-game festivities and the chaotic energy of the apparently unhinged Rossi. Italy's goalkeeper and captain Dino Zoff became the oldest player to win the World Cup, hopefully taking the edge off being depicted here as a blank-eyed Trevor Brooking mannequin.

MARCO TARDELLI
ITALY

CAMPIONI DEL MONDO!
ITALY

1986

THE HAND OF GOD

Host: Mexico

Winner:
Argentina

DENMARK

DENMARK

MICHAEL LAUDRUP

DENMARK

PREBEN ELKJAER

FRANCE

MICHEL PLATINI

I t was back to Mexico in 1986 for a tournament of classic kits, stifling heat, exquisite drama, and the mystifying and regrettable popularisation of that notable low-key-England-home-qualifier-staple: the Mexican Wave. Swings and roundabouts, isn't it?

Denmark lit up the tournament early on with some glorious football made all the prettier by their stunningly natty shirts, though the excitement of depicting them has caused us to take our eyes off the ball somewhat when it came to the humans wearing them. Sorry Michael, sorry Preben. France also brought their sartorial A-game, as modelled by midfield artisan Michel Platini.

It wasn't just the kits: this was a tournament of strong, strong looks.

It wasn't just the kits: more so than perhaps any other World Cup, this was a tournament of strong, strong looks, exemplified by Belgian teddy-boy Enzo Scifo, squinting Soviet grandmaster Igor Belanov, Brazil's lopsided nicotine enthusiast Socrates and Spain's Emilio Butragueño, who arrived after barely getting his cheekbones through Mexican customs. Beautiful guys, one and all.

IGOR BELANOV

ENZO SCIFO

SOCRATES

SPAIN

EMILIO BUTRAGUEÑO

There were some awfully lovely goals too. Brazil's unheralded right-back Josimar banana-ed an incredible long ranger past Northern Ireland's immaculately coiffured Pat Jennings, before embarking on a celebratory run of such frenzied speed that his limbs (apparently) began distorting time and space, while Mexico's Manuel Negrete scored the kind of aesthetically perfect scissor kick usually confined to bad films and even worse betting adverts. Are his limbs in proportion? Are his hands even on the correct arms? We are simply not equipped to answer.

Scotland's journey to their traditional first-round exit was enlivened considerably by the diminutive Gordon Strachan's abortive attempt to scale an advertising hoarding in celebration after scoring against West Germany. Yes, that is supposed to be him. Yes, *that* Gordon Strachan. Elsewhere in their group the uncompromisingly angry men of Uruguay arrived, kicked things, and left in a huff.

Gary Lineker, seen here looking like a waxwork dummy of himself left in a hot car.

England survived a wobbly start, embarrassed by Portugal and then being frustrated by Morocco's cherubically handsome goalkeeper Ezzaki Badou. But, fired by the goals of future potato vendor Gary Lineker, seen here looking like a waxwork dummy of himself left in a hot car, they dragged themselves to a spicy quarter-final date with recent geopolitical dance partners Argentina. And Argentina had Maradona.

Diego Armando Maradona. Never before or since has a World Cup been so dominated by one man. A squat, barrel-chested imp, tree-trunk thighs bursting from impossibly short shorts, he was Argentina's captain, their talisman, and unquestionably the best player in the world. His reputation meant he was

You know, sometimes you draw something and never quite manage to rationalise it.

JORGE BURRUCHAGA

¡CAMPEONES DEL MUNDO!

often the victim of some fairly agricultural defending, and this game was no different, with England spending the first half casually trying to elbow him into a fine paste.

Then came the moment: seizing on Steve Hodge's skewed clearance, the tiny Maradona took flight, outjumping six-foot-plus alleged professional goalkeeper Peter Shilton to jab a looping ball into the empty net with his teensy bunched fist. *The Hand of God*. Bedlam reigned but the goal bafflingly stood, a decision accepted by Shilton to this day with typical good grace. This is categorically not actually true.

Maradona's second goal was extraordinary, a magnificent slaloming run from inside his own half that would eventually be voted FIFA's Goal of the

Century. Because drawing a small man running sixty-odd yards past an entire team is, let's face it, entirely beyond us, we thought we'd go with the time-honoured 'Five Stages of Grief' coping strategy employed by Maradona's bewildered opponents. You know, sometimes you draw something and never quite manage to rationalise it.

Argentina and Diego never looked back. Another wondergoal followed in the semis against Belgium, before he released the extremely excitable Jorge Burruchaga to seal victory over West Germany in the Final. Maradona lifted the trophy high in front of 100,000 spectators at the Azteca, the greatest player at his greatest moment, and did so looking *exactly* nothing like this.

Maradona lifted the trophy high in front of 100,000 spectators at the Azteca, the greatest player at his greatest moment, and did so looking exactly nothing like this.

1990

NESSUN DORMA

Host: Italy

Winner:
Not sure, was asleep

ITALIA '90

ITALY

CIAO

...lia '90. The epicentre of ...nostalgia. For those of a ...s, let's be honest), a rose-tinted ...collective shared sporting ...s the first World Cup we have ...lection of: a glorious, hazy ...onderful introduction to a ...uld swiftly come to adore – of ...ering, bemulleted men diving, wailing and spitting their way to immortality. It was also, with the benefit of hindsight, sort of rubbish, shot through with grim cynicism and play so tediously risk-averse that the back-pass rule was subsequently brought in to liven football up a bit. Despite this, everything about it – the kits, the hair, the TV graphics, the refined bellowing of Luciano Pavarotti – can without doubt lazily be labelled as *iconic*.

ITALIA '90

ITALY

ROBERTO BAGGIO

ITALIA '90

CZECHOSLOVAKIA

TOMÁŠ SKUHRAVÝ

Sodden, sweltering, bemulleted men diving, wailing and spitting their way to immortality.

FRANÇOIS OMAM-BIYIK

The opening game saw Cameroon's *Indomitable Lions* shock the world in beating champions Argentina, though François Omam-Biyik's winner was somewhat overshadowed by the comedy violence meted out to Claudio Caniggia, who embarked on an epic length-of-the-field run while hurdling a gauntlet of the type of 'tackles' that can only be done justice by inverted commas. The coup de grace was applied by Benjamin Massing, his waist-high lunge a cinematic blur of clashing colours and a solitary flying boot. It was their second sending off of the day, and they still won. Two red cards and only

CLAUDIO CANIGGIA

BENJAMIN MASSING

JUAN CAYASSO

one goal? Yep, Italia '90 had begun alright.

Scotland, expectations perhaps tempered by all the other times things had gone very badly, could at least ease into the tournament with a straightforward first game against the minnows of Costa Rica. We'll just let your mind fill in the blanks as to how that turned out. Jim Leighton, eyebrows caked in Vaseline (don't ask us, we just draw this stuff), is well ahead of us. They duly bowed out with defeat to Brazil in a game best remembered for Murdo MacLeod having his head replaced

JIM LEIGHTON
SCOTLAND

BRANCO
BRAZIL

MURDO MACLEOD
SCOTLAND

PACKIE BONNER
REPUBLIC OF IRELAND

DAVID O'LEARY
REPUBLIC OF IRELAND

with an Adidas Etrusco Unico propelled with astonishing force by Branco, who may or may not have been dancing the Charleston.

Debutants the Republic of Ireland went on a heady run to the quarter-finals, squeaking through their group before the shoot-out heroics of the grimacing Packie Bonner and the saucily full-lipped David O'Leary edged them past Romania. Flat-capped mastermind Jack Charlton then took the team to meet the Pope ahead of their quarter-final with hosts Italy, possibly in a transparent attempt to curry divine favour. It was to no avail

JACK CHARLTON
ENGLAND

TOTO SCHILLACI

REPUBLIC OF IRELAND

however, with Italy's unheralded Golden Boot winner Toto Schillaci breaking Irish hearts, Charlton's charges having to make do with half a million people welcoming them on their return to Dublin. At least Toto looks delighted.

And so, to England who, you may have heard, had quite a time of it. Initially uninspired, they eked through a punishingly dull group stage, Mark Wright using every inch of his extensive neck to nod the critical winner to seal progress against Egypt. Belgium, reliant as ever on Enzo Scifo's still magnificent head of hair, were dispatched next via a fabulous last-minute volley from David Platt, inexplicably drawn here indulging in some unnervingly coquettish sub-Diet-Coke-advert lip biting. Shudder. A quarter-final with surprise packages Cameroon beckoned. Propelled by the goals

David Platt, inexplicably drawn here indulging in some unnervingly coquettish sub-Diet-Coke-advert lip biting.

MARK WRIGHT — ENGLAND

ENZO SCIFO — BELGIUM

DAVID PLATT — ENGLAND

of ancient totem Roger Milla and his creaking corner-flag jigs, Cameroon had followed up their opening day shock by topping their group, then mugging the heavily ringleted Colombians to become the first African nation ever to reach the last eight. England stumbled through in a sweat-drenched classic with two late Gary Lineker penalties, setting up a semi-final against, gulp, serial finalists and business-end specialists West Germany.

Cameroon: propelled by the goals of ancient totem Roger Milla and his creaking corner-flag jigs.

WEST GERMANY
RUDI VÖLLER

HOLLAND
FRANK RIJKAARD

The West Germans' route to the semis had seen an entertainingly unhygienic tear-up with the Dutch, with Frank Rijkaard applying his own special brand of 'conditioner' to Rudi Völler's poodle perm, while striker Jürgen Klinsmann had spent much of the tournament tumbling and flailing, his back theatrically arched in apparent agony, almost as if experiencing premonitions of trying to form a strike partnership with Ronny Rosenthal at Spurs a few short years later.

WEST GERMANY
JÜRGEN KLINSMANN

WEST GERMANY
JÜRGEN KLINSMANN

Striker Jürgen Klinsmann had spent much of the tournament tumbling and flailing, his back theatrically arched in apparent agony.

The match itself in Turin was unbearably tense (as a game so often is when leaving an ingrained mark on popular culture and the psyches of all who witness it), with Andreas Brehme's deflected free-kick looping over the characteristically prodigious leap of Peter Shilton to open the scoring, cancelled out late on by the inevitable Lineker equaliser. From that point on, memory dissolves into a haze of indelible, heart-breaking images, which you'll unfortunately have to view through the filter of our unskilled doodling. First, the yellow card for England's impish, effervescent genius Paul Gascoigne, ruling him out of any potential Final, his vigilant clubmate Lineker imploring the England bench to 'have a word with him.' Then the beatific smile of manager Bobby Robson, consoling the tear-stricken Gazza at the final whistle with words too heartfelt and sweet for inclusion in a book as stupid as this. And lastly, the sight of Chris Waddle's penalty disappearing high into the Turin sky, and with it England's hopes of a first World Cup Final since 1966. Ooof.

PETER SHILTON

PAUL GASCOIGNE & GARY LINEKER

BOBBY ROBSON

CHRIS WADDLE

ARGENTINA

ARGENTINA
DIEGO MARADONA

WEST GERMANY
ANDREAS BREHME

DIE WELTMEISTER!

Final was an appalling waste of everyone's time.

inal was an appalling waste of
e's time. Argentina, who had
ow clogged their way through to this
espite just two wins and five goals in
ire tournament, played for penalties
e get-go, their only contribution
gid affair being a pair of inaugural
World Cup Final red cards. A subdued
Maradona could do nothing to stop a late
Andreas Brehme penalty mercifully sealing
victory for the West Germans, shown
here celebrating both their victory and,
you'd assume, the end of one of the worst
matches in football history.

1994

Rock the Baby

Host: USA! USA! USA!

Winner: Brazil, novamente

USA — STRIKER

GERMANY — JÜRGEN KLINSMANN

For those dwelling on this side of the pond, blearily flicking on the TV at midnight to tune into USA '94 risked pickling your brain with acute sensory overload: a visually deafening festival of kaleidoscopic kits; wilting, screaming Irishmen; and voluminous, billowing goal-nets – all viewed through a blazing shimmer of summer heat, the colour and contrast settings of the entire shindig seemingly turned up to eleven. It was *brilliant*.

It began, as all the best global mega-events do, with soul megastar Diana Ross hooking a dismal penalty wide of the upright, her failure to work the goalkeeper unforgivable in the circumstances. Fellow veteran performer Roger Milla, somehow still hauling his aching bones around the pitch for Cameroon at the age of 42, fared better in becoming the World Cup's oldest ever scorer with a goal against Russia, though this was rather overshadowed by flash-in-the-pan Golden Boot winner Oleg Salenko replying with *five* of his own.

USA — DIANA ROSS

CAMEROON — ROGER MILLA

RUSSIA — OLEG SALENKO

GHEORGHE HAGI
ROMANIA

FLORIN RĂDUCIOIU
ROMANIA

BORISLAV MIKHAILOV
BULGARIA

A host of nations made unexpected splashes, with Romania able to call on both a distressed-looking Gheorghe Hagi and one Florin Răducioiu, who, with four goals in a 90s World Cup and lovely flowing hair, achieved a full house in Will-Definitely-Be-Bought-By-Harry-Redknapp Bingo. Bulgaria built their unlikely run to the last four on the bewigged goalkeeping of Borislav Mikhailov and hirsute

Răducioiu, with four goals in a 90s World Cup and lovely flowing hair, achieved a full house in Will-Definitely-Be-Bought-By-Harry-Redknapp Bingo.

TRIFON IVANOV
BULGARIA

HRISTO STOICHKOV
BULGARIA

YORDAN LETCHKOV
BULGARIA

somnambulist Trifon Ivanov, aided by the disquieting leer of Hristo Stoichkov and the wrinkled husk that was Yordan Letchkov, now our go-to image when trying to explain the effects of trying to draw the entire history of the World Cup with two very young children in the house. Letchkov was 26 at the time. Good God.

Ireland followed up their Italia '90 heroics by shocking Italy in their opener, Ray Houghton's ~~mishit~~ delicately wedged longranger leading to regrettable scenes, his celebration setting a chilling precedent for Irish goalscorers doing substandard roly-polys that would go on to appall millions.. Mexico were up next in the searing heat of Orlando, where not even the largest baseball hats in human history could cool manager Jack Charlton and his frazzled troops. A translucent Steve Staunton threatened to expire during the anthems while a temporarily insane John Aldridge vividly dispensed language every bit as colourful as Mexican 'keeper Jorge Campos' try-hard self-designed shirts. Sometimes, it really is just too hot.

RAY HOUGHTON

REP. OF IRELAND

JACK CHARLTON

ENG / REP. OF ENGLAND

STEVE STAUNTON

REP. OF IRELAND

JOHN ALDRIDGE

REP. OF IRELAND

JORGE CAMPOS

MEXICO

BRAZIL / USA
LEONARDO & TAB RAMOS

USA
ALEXI LALAS

USA
COBI JONES

The hosts, clad in kits that flirted agreeably with self-parody, gave a good account of themselves until given the elbow (literally, in the case of poor Tab Ramos) by Brazil, with denim aficionado Alexi Lalas ably backed up by the likes of Cobi Jones, whose contribution would be unfairly punished with a move to Coventry City. He looks justifiably peeved.

Elsewhere Saudi Arabia's non-plussed Saeed Al-Owairan scored the goal of the tournament, running/stumbling approximately 600 yards pursued by a troupe of comedy Belgians. Debutants Nigeria topped a difficult group, Rashidi Yekini celebrating scoring against Bulgaria by re-enacting the atomic bomb bit from *Terminator II*, while Cherubic norse assassin Tomas Brolin fired Sweden to the semis.

SAUDI ARABIA
SAEED AL-OWAIRAN

BELGIUM
MICHEL PREUD'HOMME

NIGERIA
RASHIDI YEKINI

TOMAS BROLIN
SWEDEN

DIEGO MARADONA
ARGENTINA

In bleaker events, Diego Maradona's failed drug test, hot on the heels of his lunatic celebration of his goal against Greece, provided a grimly abrupt end to his international career. You think we've exaggerated the eyes. We have not. Far grimmer still was the killing of Colombia's Andrés Escobar, murdered on his return to Bogota after his own goal against the USA contributed to Colombia's elimination. There's no fun to be had here, we can only hope our drawing has done justice to a man who by all accounts was one of the good guys.

ANDRÉS ESCOBAR
COLOMBIA

Andrés Escobar: we can only hope our drawing has done justice to a man who by all accounts was one of the good guys.

DUNGA

BRAZIL

ROMARIO

BRAZIL

The Final came down to Brazil and Italy. The *Seleção*, marshalled by the geometrically challenging head of captain Dunga, lacked the outright fantasy of their 1970 or 1982 vintages, but could still count on the goals of the (here at least) sullenly dead-eyed Romario and the baby-rocking mania of the unfortunately crazed Bebeto.

(We currently have a baby, and if someone with that expression entered our house, we absolutely would not let them rock it.) The Italians meanwhile could count on the preposterously handsome Paolo Maldini, their gameplan based entirely on allowing opposing attackers to drown in his dreamy blue eyes.

BEBETO

BRAZIL

PAOLO MALDINI

ITALY

We currently have a baby, and if someone with that expression entered our house, we absolutely would not let them rock it.

GIANLUCA PAGLIUCA

ITALY

ROBERTO BAGGIO

ITALY

The game was unfortunately a bit of a stinker, the teams spending 120 minutes failing to lay a glove on each other, save for Italy 'keeper Gianluca Pagliuca owing his right-hand post an adorable little kiss having let a mishandled powderpuff shot squirm against the woodwork. For the first time, a penalty shoot-out would decide the Final, and – in a moment that arguably signalled the end of the ponytail as an acceptable haircut – dear, sweet, beautiful Roberto Baggio, *Il Divino Codino*, spooned his shot over the bar to give Brazil victory. As the Brazilians cavorted, Baggio stared crestfallen down at the turf, the world echoing to the anguished cries of Diadora shareholders everywhere. Oh, Bobby.

CAMPEÕES DA COPA DO MUNDO!

BRAZIL

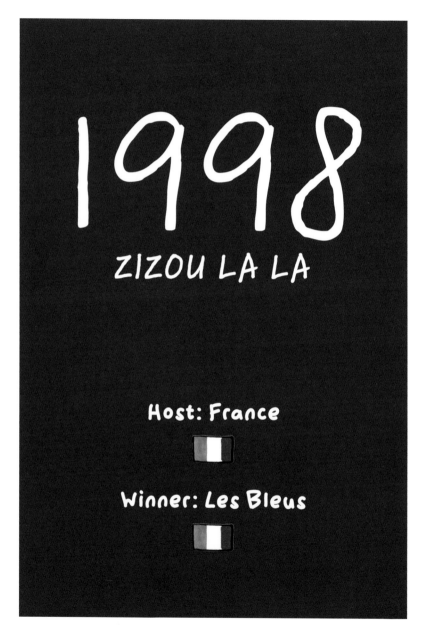

1998

ZIZOU LA LA

Host: France

Winner: Les Bleus

DES LYNAM
IRELAND

FOOTIX
FRANCE

'**S**houldn't you be at work?' enquired the BBC's Des Lynam with a knowing raise of the eyebrow as England, returning from their holidays, kicked off their France '98 campaign against Tunisia. A zinger of an opening line no doubt (though of course *technically* we should actually have been at school), providing the kind of embedded mental anchor-point necessary for every subsequent detail of a tournament to still be lodged worryingly in your head decades later. Most people probably don't ruin it by trying to cackhandedly draw it all, though.

The *Reggae Boyz* of Jamaica made their World Cup bow, the terrifying Robbie Earle seen here saluting the majesty of their beautiful, remarkably-difficult-to-get-hold-of-on-eBay shirts. Their closest rivals in the fashion stakes were the lovely Aztec-inspired efforts worn by Mexico, whose Cuauhtémoc Blanco inspired a million clumsy playground imitators with the 'Cuauhtemiña' or 'Blanco Bounce', gripping the ball between his insteps and bunny-hopping over challenges to the amazement of his crudely drawn opponents. Look, look how amazed they are.

ROBBIE EARLE
JAMAICA

CUAUHTÉMOC BLANCO
MEXICO

Blanco, bunny-hopping over challenges to the amazement of his crudely drawn opponents.

CRAIG BURLEY
SCOTLAND

Scotland, you will have no doubt guessed, dutifully trudged out in the first round, their experience best summed up by Craig Burley here, immortalised moments after equalising against Norway and subsequently being told he'll be the last Scotsman to score at a major finals for twenty-three years.

In super-fun geopolitics news, Iran lulled ideological rivals USA into a false sense of security with a pre-match gift of some pretty flowers, before vanquishing the Great Satan with a late winner from the oddly joyless Mehdi Mahdavikia. Nobody's fool, Kasey Keller's face accurately reflects this alarming foreign policy implications of this development.

MEHDI MAHDAVIKIA
IRAN

KASEY KELLER
UNITED STATES

TONI POLSTER
AUSTRIA

LUIS HERNÁNDEZ
MÉXICO

TARIBO WEST
NIGERIA

ROMANIA

JAY-JAY OKOCHA
NIGERIA

EDGAR DAVIDS
NETHERLANDS

Happily for any substandard artists looking for easily recognisable features to shambolically depict, it was an *excellent* tournament for hair. The greying temples of Austrian die-hard mulleteer Toni Polster, the feathery peroxide nonsense of Luis Hernández of Mexico, and Taribo West outdoing Nigeria teammate Jay-Jay Okocha's curiously ginger dye-job with a set of dancing, prancing, braided pigtails. Surpassing them all though were Romania, who celebrated winning their first two games by bleaching their hair blonde *en masse*, infuriating commentators the world over. After their winning run ended in their next game against Tunisia, manager Anghel Iordănescu claimed 'we have angered God.' Bit dramatic, maybe.

England pottered to a second-round meeting with Argentina where – after an early exchange of penalties from wind tunnel tester Gabriel Batistuta and the monstrously-handed Alan Shearer – they took the lead with a solo very-good-but-not-quite-as-good-as-you-remember-it goal from teenaged whiskey buff Michael Owen. Javier Zanetti equalised before dear, be-curtained David Beckham's errant, waggling leg earned him a very silly red card, depicted by us here with at best rudimentary competence. An unbearably tense hour followed, at the end of which England finally stopped resisting the inevitable and got on the with serious business of going out on penalties. Oh, England...

The quarter-finals saw Brazil edge out Denmark, Brian Laudrup's 'draw me like one of your Danish guys' post-goal debauchery proving far too tempting an invitation for us to turn down, while the Netherlands' Dennis Bergkamp plucked a 70-yard Frank de Boer punt out of the sky to score an astonishing last-minute winner against Argentina.

We have come to the conclusion that some people are just fundamentally undrawable.

We've had two goes at Dennis here in a vain attempt to do this moment justice, and have come to the conclusion that some people are just fundamentally undrawable.

Debutants Croatia swatted aside Germany to make the last four, inspired by dishevelled midfield schemer Robert Prosinečki (just a cigarette away from his Pompey pomp) and the goals of Davor Šuker, who nabbed the Golden Boot ahead

of the extremely caffeinated Christian Vieri. Hosts France awaited, having squeaked past Italy on penalties, the fickle Gods of footballing fate clearly having been charmed by goalkeeper Fabien Barthez's pre-match lucky ritual of letting Laurent Blanc kiss him on his extremely bald head (though our drawing looks more like he's trying to *inflate* the poor man). A thrilling match – marred/further enlivened by the

SLAVEN BILIĆ
CROATIA

LILIAN THURAM
FRANCE

RONALDO
BRAZIL

playacting of Croatia's Slaven Bilić, seen here apparently smelling something terrible on Blanc's hand – was ultimately settled by an unlikely brace from Lilian Thuram, whose iconic goal celebration we have somehow reduced to a crude image of a quizzical man picking his nose.

France's opponents in the Final would be champions Brazil, who – in a theme we'll revisit – somehow found themselves at the pointy end of a World Cup despite not really having done a great deal. They *did* however have Ronaldo, *O Fenômeno*, a force of nature at just 21 years old and with the world at his conspicuously Nike-clad feet. What followed has never quite been satisfactorily explained

but, in the hours before the Final, Ronaldo apparently suffered a convulsive fit, was taken to hospital, discharged, removed from the starting XI, and then amid widespread bewilderment immediately reinstated. Rumours swirled implying interference from officials and sponsors and it was all very unfunny indeed. Ronaldo, understandably, was barely a shadow of his normal self as France's 'Rainbow Team' strolled to a handsome 3-0 win with a pair of ominously powerful headers from Zinedine Zidane, with Zizou lifting the trophy high while looking, apparently, like some kind of sentient peanut. Ah well, we tried.

LES CHAMPIONS DU MONDE!

ZINEDINE ZIDANE
FRANCE

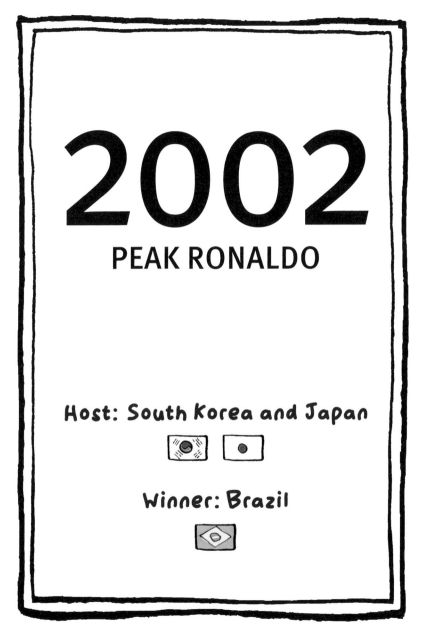

2002

PEAK RONALDO

Host: South Korea and Japan

Winner: Brazil

ATO, KAZ & NIK

ROY KEANE

PAPA BOUBA DIOP

EL HADJI DIOUF

FIFA's travelling circus journeyed to Asia for the first time in 2002, with Japan and South Korea sharing hosting duties in a tournament dominated by surprise results, endless controversy and, in our house at least, the unsettling queasiness brought on by trying to watch nail-biting elite-level sport while eating Coco Pops for breakfast.

The fun began before a ball had even been kicked, Ireland's preparations being somewhat undermined by notoriously easy-going skipper Roy Keane flouncing out of a pre-tournament training camp, on his way vividly advising manager Mick McCarthy to carry out some frankly unlikely-sounding procedures involving the human anatomy and a 6kg trophy. Keane spent the tournament walking his newly-famous dog Triggs, the '**Saipan Incident**' as it became known so dividing the Irish nation that its Wikipedia page thrillingly lists among its outcomes a 'prolonged national self-examination.' You don't get that with Séamus Coleman.

The opening game saw Senegal set the tone for a tournament of underdog triumphs by humbling reigning champions France, the winner bundled home by the leviathan frame of Papa Bouba Diop. France – perhaps unnerved by the upsetting visage of saliva enthusiast El Hadji Diouf – proceeded to slouch to the bottom of their group and departed without scoring a goal, a spectacular implosion that in no way foreshadowed future events.

RONALDINHO

RIVALDO

Meanwhile Brazil, packed with stars and with the unsatisfactorily-nicknamed 'Triple R' forward line of Ronaldo, Rivaldo and Ronaldinho, briefly became the most unpopular team in World Cup history thanks to a moment of jaw-dropping scumbaggery from Rivaldo, who collapsed to the turf clutching his face after Turkey's Hakan Ünsal pinged a ball off his thigh.

As with all World Cups, there were a wide variety of handsome men, including but not limited to Belgium's recently woken Marc Wilmots, large-faced goalkeeping maverick José Luis Chilavert of Paraguay, and the USA's Claudio Reyna, who quite simply has far too many features for one human face. Meanwhile in celebration news, Sweden's Henrik Larsson poked out a frighteningly large tongue, Jon Dahl Tomasson of Denmark apparently took up yodelling, while Robbie Keane's clanking, ungainly cartwheel-into-abject-forward-roll mish-mash impressed nobody.

MARC WILMOTS

JOSÉ LUIS CHILAVERT

CLAUDIO REYNA

Robbie Keane's clanking, ungainly cartwheel-into abject-forward-roll mish-mash impressed nobody.

Both host nations thrived. Japan, led by winking fashionista Hidetoshi Nakata, topped their group in style, a feat that was more than matched by their South Korean counterparts. Embarking on a massively unlikely run to the semi-finals, they first edged out Italy in a match officiated by future convicted heroin smuggler and all-round paragon of virtue Byron Moreno – pictured here sending off Francesco Totti in the midst of a *very normal*

refereeing performance. Italian rage spilled over, South Korea's Golden Goal-scoring Ahn Jung-hwan being sacked by his Italian club side Perugia, an event captured here in our painfully over-literal depiction. Spain were dispatched next, bested by two *ever-*

so-slightly generous linesman's flags and the shoot-out heroics of goalkeeper Lee Woon-jae, nicknamed 'the spider-hand' in his native South Korea. Did each glove conceal eight fingers? We may never know. Look at poor Fernando Hierro, his brain broken by the injustice of it all.

Look at poor Fernando Hierro, his brain broken by the injustice of it all.

England's David Beckham, faced once more with serial antagonists Argentina, walloped home a redemptive penalty to settle a fraught group stage encounter, the sheer catharsis of the moment apparently sending the faux-hawked megastar at least 70 per cent feral. Victory over Denmark followed, hence the fury of the snarling Thomas Gravesen. (Let us tell you: it's a sobering thought when sitting down to draw Thomas Gravesen that he might one day see the drawing and then find out who drew it and then find out where we live and then come round and do Thomas Gravesen things to us. Brrrr.) Brazil awaited in the quarter-finals, where ponytailed goalkeeper and professional Yorkshireman David Seaman was cruelly embarrassed by Ronaldinho's outlandish free-kick. There was no way back for England, despite the flamboyant flip-flapper's subsequent red card and the presence on the pitch throughout of *Danny Mills*.

RÜŞTÜ REÇBER

PIERLUIGI COLLINA

RONALDO

The semis saw the South Koreans' luck finally run out against Germany and the hooting, hollering Michael Ballack, while Brazil squeezed past Turkey's goalkeeping maniac Rüştü Reçber and his scary-dary warpaint. The Final would be overseen by the piercing glare of Pierluigi Collina, undoubtedly the best referee on the planet and *still* the only ref to grace the cover of a major football video game – a fact that will remain true at least until the release of *'Michael Oliver's VAR Officiator II'* or the inexorable heat death of the universe, whichever arrives first. The decider saw Ronaldo, revelling in possibly the most unconvincing haircut in human (never mind football) history, lay to rest the traumas of 1998 with both goals as Brazil brushed aside the Germans, to the consternation of walking bellow Oliver Kahn, whose surname should have about sixteen As judging by this drawing of him. Kaaaaaaaaaaaaaaaahn.

OLIVER KAHN

CAMPEÕES DA COPA DO MUNDO!

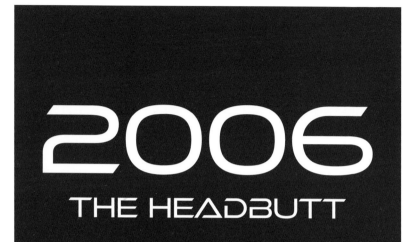

2006

THE HEADBUTT

Host: Germany

Winner: Italy

ARGENTINA
LIONEL MESSI

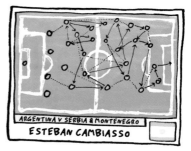

ARGENTINA V SERBIA & MONTENEGRO
ESTEBAN CAMBIASSO

ARGENTINA
MAXI RODRÍGUEZ

Germany was the venue for World Cup 2006, a tournament which promised much: welcoming hosts, a last hurrah for titans like Ronaldo and Zidane, and England's extremely promising and not at all cursed 'Golden Generation' blossoming into a genuine international force. Ho hum.

Argentina made the early running, briefly threatening to become the best team in the history of football with a *beautiful* 6-0 demolition of Serbia & Montenegro, the crowning glory of which was Esteban Cambiasso finishing off a passing move that had started sometime in late 2003. Even that was arguably eclipsed by Maxi Rodríguez's ludicrous volley against Mexico, poor Maxi depicted here as a squat homunculus in a drawing we fully expect will result in legal action.

Notable impacts on our brains were made by Australian goal-cube John Aloisi, braying eyesore Hernán Crespo of Argentina, and Ecuador's José Luis Perlaza, who hopefully

Poor Maxi, depicted here as a squat homunculus in a drawing we fully expect will result in legal action.

AUSTRALIA
JOHN ALOISI

ARGENTINA
HERNÁN CRESPO

ECUADOR
JOSÉ LUIS PERLAZA

got a discount when purchasing three haircuts for the price of one. Elsewhere Ronaldo – who in this confusing crossover period we are obliged to refer to as *original* Ronaldo – made himself the top scorer in World Cup history with a goal against Ghana despite being arguably past his peak, though judging by our drawing we should probably say *inarguably*. Meanwhile English referee Graham Poll had something of a time, issuing Croatia's baffled and bleary-eyed Josip Šimunić with not one, not two, but *three* yellow cards in a single game. At least he seems to have found time to get his nails done.

BRAZIL
RONALDO

CROATIA
JOSIP ŠIMUNIĆ

ENGLAND
GRAHAM POLL

BATTLE OF NUREMBERG
LUÍS FIGO &
VAN BOMMEL

BATTLE OF NUREMBERG
VAN BRONCKHORST
& DECO

Now, there's a school of thought that no World Cup game can truly be considered a classic until it has its own exhaustive Wikipedia entry. With that in mind we present: the '**Battle of Nuremberg**', a spectacularly fractious second round tie between Portugal and the Netherlands, replete with sixteen yellow cards, four sendings-off, Luís Figo attempting to restore karmic balance to the cosmos by headbutting serial irritant Mark van Bommel, and the glorious sight of dismissed clubmates Deco and Giovanni van Bronckhorst sat forlornly together, watching the carnage unfold like recently chastised schoolboys. Referee Valentin Ivanov, pictured here having a wonderful time, has our undying gratitude for nurturing such high-calibre nonsense.

RUSSIA
VALENTIN IVANOV

Referee Valentin Ivanov, pictured here having a wonderful time, has our undying gratitude for nurturing such high-calibre nonsense.

ENGLAND
PETER CROUCH

ENGLAND
WAYNE ROONEY

PORTUGAL
RICARDO CARVALHO

Portugal followed up these frivolities with a similarly cantankerous meeting with England, whose waltz through the group stage was indebted to elongated curio Peter Crouch indulging in some unsolicited scalp massage against Trinidad & Tobago. The quarter-final itself saw England's prodigal man-child Wayne Rooney sent off after clumsily rearranging the nether regions of Ricardo Carvalho, our drawings of which pose many important questions, chief among them why does Carvalho have the proportions of a six-year-old child, and why has Rooney's head been replaced by some kind of squash? We need answers. Clubmate Cristiano Ronaldo's sly wink after Rooney's red card and the seemingly predestined penalty shoot-out defeat that followed were enough to boil the blood – and quite possibly other bodily fluids too.

Italy and Germany played out an enthralling, epic semi-final, Fabio Grosso harnessing the prevailing 1982-redux vibes with a glorious (if horribly drawn) Tardelli-evoking sprint after curling Italy ahead in

PORTUGAL
CRISTIANO RONALDO

Why does Carvalho have the proportions of a six-year-old child, and why has Rooney's head been replaced by some kind of squash?

ITALY
FABIO GROSSO

ITALY
ALESSANDRO DEL PIERO

GERMANY
MIROSLAV KLOSE

FRANCE
ZINEDINE ZIDANE

ITALY
MARCO MATERAZZI

the 119th minute. Alessandro Del Piero and his oddly boneless-looking hand sealed victory moments later, with Germany's Golden Boot-winning Miroslav Klose looking on in frozen, abject horror. Italy's reward was a place in the Final. A Final against France: the France of Zinedine Yazid Zidane.

Subdued as France staggered out of their group, the knock-out stages had seen Zidane at his imperious best, as he dismantled Spain, Brazil and Portugal with goals, assists, and those signature pirouettes which are an excellent way of tearing something if tried at the level of football *we're* familiar with. Having announced his intention to retire after the tournament, the Final would be Zidane's last game as a professional, the stars seemingly aligned for arguably the greatest player of his generation to go out on top of the world. What could possibly go wrong?

The operatic madness of the Final itself may never be surpassed. With the scores at one-all deep into extra-time, Italy's shrinking violet Marco Materazzi yelled *something* at the passing Zidane. Zizou, a man who two hours earlier had had sufficient ice in his veins to **panenka a penalty in off the bar**

against the best goalkeeper in the world in a World Cup Final, took something of an exception to this, and proceeded to banish Materazzi to the land of wind and ghosts by attempting to plant his massive cranium through the Italian's ribcage. It was a jaw-dropping moment, almost certainly a good bit more dramatic than our abject doodlings can convey. Zidane, *massively* sent off, stalked past the World Cup trophy, then watched on helplessly as Italy triumphed on penalties to the delight of a honking Gianluigi Buffon. Oh, Zizou. It could have been the ultimate dénouement to one of the all-time great careers. Instead, we had to watch Gennaro Gattuso cavorting with his bum out.

2010

Hooooonnnnkkkk

Host: South Africa

Winner: Spain

BAFANA BAFANA

ENG   ROBERT GREEN

'**G**oal Bafana Bafana! Goal for South Africa! Goal for all Africa!' bellowed telly-man Peter Drury as Siphiwe Tshabalala lashed in the opening goal of the 2010 World Cup, sparking delirious scenes and a fresh chorus of vuvuzelas across Johannesburg and beyond. Was he right? Africa had had plenty of World Cup moments before, as fans of Cameroon, Nigeria, Algeria, Morocco and more could attest. You kind of knew what he meant though: a tournament on African soil was long overdue, and you wanted it to be a *blast*.

No such fun was had by England. From the moment Rob Green let Clint Dempsey's limp longshot squirm over the line in their opener against the USA, their campaign became something of a nightmarish fever dream. An atrocious stalemate with Algeria followed, with Wayne Rooney – who really hasn't come out of this well – taking exception to the displeasure voiced by the travelling fans to

USA   CLINT DEMPSEY

USA LANDON DONOVAN

ENG WAYNE ROONEY

dispense some colourful wisdom down the nearest camera lens. (Fun fact: we watched this game in a near-deserted beachside café in South Wales with several other Welsh people and one lone Englander. On the introduction of Peter Crouch as an 84th minute substitute, he calmly walked out of the café, across the sand and directly into the sea.)

It could have been worse: France disappeared up their own exhaust pipe, a series of petty squabbles, grievances and internal implosions resulting in the team publicly abandoning a training session to sit grumpily on their team bus. With that in mind, we drew a bus. Buses are easier than people. Hurrah for buses.

FRANCE

With that in mind, we drew a bus.
Buses are easier than people.
Hurrah for buses.

Now, every now and again we draw something that begs the question: how did this happen? Our attempt at poor Diego Forlan falls well within this category, a bulging mad-necked gargoyle where in reality stands a buffed and handsome Adonis. Diego, if you're reading, we really like you and are very sorry. Slovakia's Róbert Vittek fares little better, matched in the unsettlingly-protruding-tongue stakes by Argentina's bedraggled Gonzalo Higuaín, while Gervinho's megalithic forehead is now the thing we see when we close our eyes at night.

Gervinho's megalithic forehead is now the thing we see when we close our eyes at night.

GER MANUEL NEUER

ENG FRANK LAMPARD

England's fun continued in their last-16 meeting with Germany, where Frank Lampard's pot-shot hit the bar before bouncing a good foot over the unnervingly hovering Manuel Neuer's goal-line. The goal wasn't given, much to Lampard's pop-eyed chagrin, and England were duly administered a 4-1 skelping by their terrifyingly youthful opponents (youthful that is at least until Golden Boot-winning Thomas Müller apparently opened the Ark of the Covenant).

Elsewhere Ghana came within a piece of self-parodically evil Luis Suárez dirtbaggery of becoming the first ever African nation to reach the semi-finals, the comically

GER BASTIAN SCHWEINSTEIGER

GER THOMAS MÜLLER

GHA ASAMOAH GYAN

URU LUIS SUÁREZ

NED WESLEY SNEIJDER

villainous Uruguayan palming a late goal-bound effort over the bar to save his side's skin and enrage an entire continent. Poor, wrinkled Asamoah Gyan thumped the resultant penalty against the bar, sending the red-carded Suárez cackling up and down the tunnel. Suárez's crimes are immortalised here in our first ever attempt at drawing an archetypal goalmouth scramble, which we have entitled **'International Footballer Soup'**.

The Final came down to Spain and the Netherlands, the Dutch route to the decider built on the goals of rosy-cheeked funster Wesley Sneijder and the combative engine-room skulduggery of automated fouling machines Mark van Bommel and Nigel de Jong, **Total Football** now something of a distant memory. Facing them would be Spain's well-grooved tiki-taka artists, anchored by the 8000 BC stylings of Carles Puyol and augmented by the firepower

NED MARK VAN BOMMEL

ESP CARLES PUYOL

ESP DAVID VILLA

ESP XABI ALONSO

NED NIGEL DE JONG

of David Villa, famously owner of the last remaining soul-patch in international sport. The match itself was a grisly spectacle, the lone 'highlight' being Nigel de Jong somehow – in a match that saw *fourteen* yellow cards – escaping sanction after attempting to drive an entire human leg through the torso of poor, mangled Xabi Alonso. A late, late goal from a passionate – if terrifying – Andrés Iniesta was enough to give Spain their first World Cup win, their post-game celebrations only slightly marred by our subsequent attempts to draw them.

ESP ANDRÉS INIESTA

¡CAMPEONES DEL MUNDO!

ESP XAVI

2014

Humbled Hosts

Host: Brazil

Winner: Not Brazil!

ROBIN VAN PERSIE

IKER CASILLAS

NANI

With Brazil the welcoming hosts for World Cup 2014, it was difficult to not get drawn in by all the usual cliches: Samba! Carnival! Copacabana! Joga bonito! Month-long host-nation psychodrama! Ah, yes, we'll come back to that.

Spain's defence of their crown was surprisingly catastrophic, the mysteriously levitating Robin van Persie inspiring an opening 5-1 tanking by the Netherlands, much to the dismay of forlorn, oven-mitted Iker Casillas. Much-fancied Portugal likewise bowed out early, a shame after Nani had gone to all that trouble with his hair. England meanwhile were just breathtakingly terrible – their one contribution to the tournament being manager Roy Hodgson's immortalisation as a 'before and after' meme.

ROY HODGSON

ROY HODGSON

England's one contribution to the tournament being manager Roy Hodgson's immortalisation as a 'before and after' meme.

TIM CAHILL

DF ASSOU-EKOTTO
& MOUKANDJO

Elsewhere in the group stage, pouting Australian vision Tim Cahill crashed home arguably the best ever World Cup volley by a former Millwall player, while Cameroonian Smart Car appreciator Benoit Assou-Ekotto headbutted teammate Benjamin Moukandjo, the impact hopefully lessened by Disco Benny's luxurious head of hair. Indeed, it was a vintage World Cup for follicles, between the dependably chaotic thatch of Belgium's Marouane Fellaini, glum Mario Balotelli and his half-arsed mohawk, and the single lonely strand sprouting from the scalp of Argentina's Rodrigo Palacio. Of note: we only had to draw the back of Rodrigo's head, and we still couldn't get the ears right.

Indeed, it was a vintage World Cup for follicles

MF MAROUANE FELLAINI

FW MARIO BALOTELLI

FW RODRIGO PALACIO

LUIS SUÁREZ

TIM HOWARD

To the surprise of absolutely no-one, Luis Suárez disgraced himself for the second World Cup in a row, eschewing common-or-garden foul play this time in favour of sinking his generously proportioned teeth into Giorgio Chiellini's shoulder. Drawing this left us feeling more than a bit queasy, the sight of Suárez's lone eye rolling back into his head in apparent carnivorous ecstasy not an easy one to get over.

USA goalkeeper Tim Howard earned himself a place in the history books after making a record fifteen (*cough*, fairly routine, *end cough*) saves against Belgium, an achievement that probably – if our drawing of him is at all accurate – owed at least a little to the ever-loving state of the man. His heroics were more than matched by the Netherlands' substitute 'keeper and lumpen scoundrel Tim Krul, whose extravagant

TIM KRUL

BRYAN RUIZ

FRED

ALEXIS SÁNCHEZ

shootout chicanery denied dot-eyed Bryan Ruiz and his Costa Rica team a place in the last four.

The story of the 2014 World Cup though, really, was the story of Brazil. Some sixty-four years on from the traumas of the *Maracanaço*, they were hosts again. Worse still, they were *favourites* again. Their team was in truth something of an odd bunch – the undoubted quality of Thiago Silva, Dani Alves, and Neymar on the one hand, cuddly blunt instrument Fred on the other. Winning the World Cup on home soil wouldn't be easy but, desperate to bury the ghosts of 1950 and with an expectant nation at their back, anything was possible.

Instead, though, it all just got a bit *much*.

After flattering to deceive in the group stage, they edged past the Chile of Alexis Sánchez (pictured scarring millions by doing *whatever this thing involving his shorts is*) to book a quarter-final date with Colombia, which is where things started to go a bit wrong. The Colombians had taken the tournament by storm, star turn James Rodríguez charming the world with his smiling face and infectious bum-wiggle,

Alexis Sánchez (pictured scarring millions by doing *whatever this thing involving his shorts is*)

JAMES RODRÍGUEZ

NEYMAR

DAVID LUIZ

plus a truly *mind-bending* volley against Uruguay. Brazil's response was to spend the entire match shoeing him to the turf at every opportunity, the Colombians eventually dishing out a little in return when Juan Camilo Zúñiga planted his knee into Neymar's back, ending the impish waif's tournament. David Luiz was able to dodge just enough rakes to smash home a free-kick to seal victory (before, as our drawing shows with rare accuracy, getting slightly overexcited) but Brazil, rattled by the injury to their talisman, looked very much like a team on the edge.

To the semi-final then. Germany versus Brazil. The Estádio Mineirão. 58,000 fans, plus a planet watching on TV. Anthems. Emotion. Too much emotion. David Luiz, boggle-eyed, clutching absent Neymar's shirt. Tears. Deep breaths. The fans. The atmosphere. The *expectation*. Kick-off. And then... Müller after just 11 minutes. Klose after 23. Then Kroos. Kroos again. Then Khedira. 5-0 after half an hour. A battering.

MIROSLAV KLOSE

TONI KROOS

THE MINEIRAÇO

MARCELO

Javier Mascherano quite literally tore himself a new one while denying Arjen Robben with a last-ditch arse-tackle.

A mauling. A defenestration. The single biggest humiliation in football history. For *Maracanaço*, read *Mineiraço*. It finishes 7-1. *Seven*. One.

Oof.

The other, comparatively sane semi-final saw Argentina's Javier Mascherano quite

literally tearing himself a new one while denying the Netherland's Arjen Robben with a last-ditch arse-tackle, Arjen at least seeming to see the funny side, the callous scamp. Poor, sore Javier's reward was a place in the Final which, not for the first time, was several shades

JAVIER MASCHERANO

ARJEN ROBBEN

less dramatic than pretty much everything that had gone before, the tournament itself seemingly drained by the madness of Brazil's implosion. After nearly two hours of not a great deal happening, artistic travesty Mario Götze snaffled a late winner for Germany, a bereft Lionel Messi left with the scant consolation of being awarded the Golden Ball, a consolation we have promptly ruined by making him look like a sad child mourning a deflated balloon.

LIONEL MESSI

Messi was left with the scant consolation of being awarded the Golden Ball, a consolation we have promptly ruined by making him look like a sad child mourning a deflated balloon.

MARIO GÖTZE

DIE WELTMEISTER!

2018

SOUTHGATE, YOU'RE THE ONE

Host: Russia

Winner: France

EDINSON CAVANI

GERMANY

Russia. The 2018 World Cup was in Russia. Russia. A long-winded and transparently crooked bidding process, a process *after which almost everyone involved got arrested*, awarded the World Cup to Russia. Russia. *That* Russia. Putin's Russia. State-sponsored doping's Russia. *Russia*. Oh FIFA, don't you go changing. *That being said*, our brief *is* to draw this nonsense, no matter how unpalatable, so buckle up and let's see if things can get much worse than this scribble of husky Uruguayan dreamboat Edinson Cavani. Sigh.

The group stage saw plenty of fun and games: after years of tiresome 'honestly, he's good enough to play in midfield!' punditry, it was satisfying indeed to witness German goalkeeper Manuel Neuer – cosplaying as Lothar Matthäus ten yards outside the *opposition's* box – having his pocket picked against South Korea, the ever-smiley Son Heung-Min racing away to dump the holders out in the first round. Despite a couple of goals, Mohamed Salah and his lovely, happy – if asymmetric – face couldn't prevent Egypt from joining them.

MOHAMED SALAH

Despite a couple of goals, Mohamed Salah and his lovely, happy – if asymmetric – face couldn't prevent Egypt from joining them.

CRISTIANO RONALDO

NEYMAR

AHMED MUSA

Shy, retiring Cristiano Ronaldo blootered a hat-trick against Spain, the Portuguese's wearying pre-free-kick routine – imagine a thumb, with thighs, doing Pilates – captured here in distressingly vivid detail. Elsewhere, Brazil weren't great, their only contribution of note being Neymar's frankly extraordinary range of balletically meme-worthy tumbles.

It was a stellar tournament for natty kits, with Nigeria's mid-yawn Ahmed Musa modelling what was undoubtedly the pick of the bunch, run close by the Pringle-fied diamonds of Belgium's shirt, seen here just about keeping a desiccated Eden Hazard upright. Handsome humans were everywhere too, exemplified by the hosts' wasp-chewing Denis Cheryshev, Australia's inscrutable woodsman Mile Jedinak

EDEN HAZARD

DENIS CHERYSHEV

MILE JEDINAK

DOMAGOJ VIDA

and Croatia's Domagoj Vida, happily free to play after escaping from that big painting in *Ghostbusters II*.

And then there was Michy. Poor Michy Batshuayi. He just wanted to have some fun. After all, his Belgium teammate Adnan Januzaj had just scored a very nice goal, and the ball had come trundling back out of the net towards him, and he was feeling all happy and fizzy and excited, and he just wanted to *show it*, he just wanted to share in the joy. 'I know,' he thought, 'I'll do that thing people

do sometimes just after a goal has been scored and kick the ball back into the net. It'll be great! I might even shout "**and another!**" as I do it' Poor Michy. Poor, poor Michy. In a moment of distilled, unalloyed slapstick perfection, our hero walloped the ball not back into the net, but instead into the post, from whence it bounced with astounding velocity straight back into the side of his face. Please, FIFA: take this moment, cast it in gold, and replace the World Cup with it.

MICHY BATSHUAYI

MICHY BATSHUAYI

Michy wasn't the only man to feel that burning sensation that comes with having the entirety of planet Earth watch you humiliate yourself: spare a thought too for Iran's Milad Mohammadi who, a goal down with just twenty seconds to go in his nation's clash with Spain, decided now was the time to unveil his hitherto unseen, quite possibly never-practiced *somersault throw-in*. It's entirely possible that what followed represents the single greatest moment in the history of the World Cup, if not of all human endeavour. Suffice to say its majesty was fully deserving of no less than *six* very, very bad drawings.

It's entirely possible that what followed represents the single greatest moment in the history of the World Cup, if not of all human endeavour.

GARETH SOUTHGATE

HARRY KANE

YERRY MINA

England, in a jarring departure from the prevailing vibes of more or less every World Cup since 1990, were actually quite *good*.

Meanwhile England, in a jarring departure from the prevailing vibes of more or less every World Cup since 1990, were A) a thoroughly likeable bunch and B) actually quite *good*, presenting a conundrum for anyone living *in* England, but not necessarily *from* England, but who didn't *mind* England, but didn't really *support* England, but who because of a sequence of terrible events found themselves compelled to *draw* England... look, it was a confusing time, is all we're saying. Overseen by mild-mannered waistcoat cognoscente Gareth Southgate and led by the goals of gawping, Golden Boot-bothering skipper Harry Kane, England's troublingly amiable bunch strolled to a last-16 meeting with Colombia, their team-spirit and evident camaraderie carrying a thoroughly charmed nation with them. A late, late goal from the alarmingly puckered Yerry Mina denied them victory, only for England – in another break with established tradition – to actually go and *win* a penalty shoot-out for goodness' sake, the decisive kick scuffed home by allotment devotee

ERIC DIER

"IT'S COMING HOME..."

LUKA MODRIĆ

and all-round-hero Eric Dier. Sweden were dispatched next, the sheer volume of flying pints seeing beer briefly replace 'light drizzle' as the nation's primary form of precipitation.

England were *good*. Croatia in the semi-final, however, were better. Despite leading early, England were ultimately undone by the metronomic scuttling of anthropomorphised cartoon mouse Luka Modrić, who tied England's outmatched midfield in knots to lead the Croatians to their first ever Final. England departed, heads held high for what felt like the first time in a long time, free to bask in the glory of some truly, genuinely sublime post-tournament montages, and safe in the knowledge that no fan would ever look at an inflatable pool unicorn the same way again.

Beer briefly replaced 'light drizzle' as the nation's primary form of precipitation.

HARRY MAGUIRE

ENGLAND

KYLIAN MBAPPÉ

BENJAMIN PAVARD

MARIO MANDŽUKIĆ

Croatia's opponents in the Final would be France, who had seen off Argentina in a classic punctuated by the roadrunner speed of the cruelly distorted Kylian Mbappé and the heroics of Benjamin Pavard, whose wondrous strike was approximately 4,000 times more impressive than this stick-man-doing-an-Arabesque attempt at a likeness would have you believe. Despite the best (and worst) efforts of Mario Mandžukić (who scored at both ends, see?), France ultimately proved just too good for Croatia on the day, goals from a recently tranquilized Antoine Griezmann and shrieking abomination Paul Pogba helping France to their second World Cup win. Captain Hugo Lloris, rendered here an indistinct smudge, lifted the trophy high, with a force of feeling we hope to emulate when throwing our pencils in a canal at the conclusion of this appalling book.

ANTOINE GRIEZMANN

LES CHAMPIONS DU MONDE!

PAUL POGBA

2022

JUST DESERTS

Host: Qatar

Winner: The money men

And so to Qatar 2022. *The future.* Another World Cup, another dubiously chosen venue more or less guaranteed to elicit a weary sigh and, of course, another set of shambolic renderings from two idiots with more pens than sense.

At the time of writing/doodling, we have no idea what will happen at Qatar 2022. If you received this book as an unwanted gift soon after its release, you could be staring in slack-jawed awe at your TV as our (admittedly bold) prediction of a surprisingly dominant Wales sweeping all before them comes to pass before your very eyes. Alternatively, if you fished it from a skip some years later (as seems more likely), you'll be able to look back at this selection of grotesque potential trophy-ravishers, point at one and say 'That's

more or less what happened. Just a bit less scary-looking.'

We don't know what will happen. All we know is that instead of watching it and enjoying it like normal people, we'll be ankle-deep in pencil shavings, staring at our laps, crayons in our shaking, rubbish hands, having a thoroughly strange and wonderful time.

WALES

We don't know what will happen.
All we know is that instead of
watching it and enjoying it like normal
people, we'll be ankle-deep in pencil
shavings, staring at our laps, crayons
in our shaking, rubbish hands,
having a thoroughly strange and
wonderful time.

If we can do it, anyone can.

Draw your own crap World Cup moment and share with us on Twitter @CheapPanini

Uruguay 1930

Italy 1934

France 1938

Brazil 1950

Switzerland 1954

Sweden 1958

Chile 1962

England 1966

Mexico 1970

West Germany 1974

ARGENTINA 78

Argentina 1978

ESPAÑA 82

Spain 1982

Mexico 1986

ITALIA-90

Italy 1990

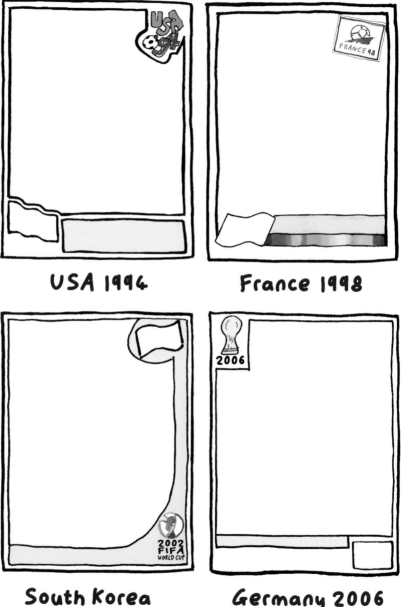

USA 1994

France 1998

South Korea
& Japan 2002

Germany 2006

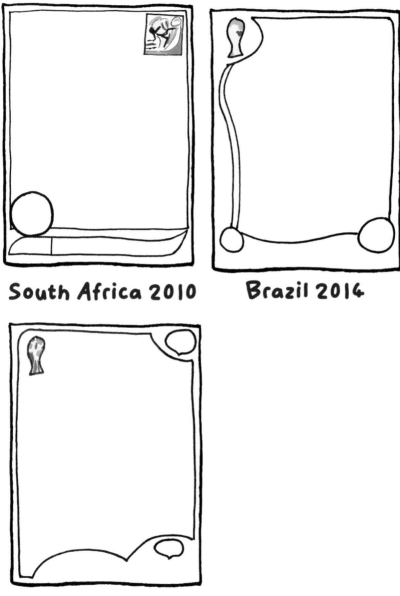

South Africa 2010

Brazil 2014

France 2018